ONLY

a memoir

WAY TO

through scripture

GRACE

DAVID DALY

AND DAWN MERROW

AMBASSADOR INTERNATIONAL
GREENVILLE, SOUTH CAROLINA & BELFAST, NORTHERN IRELAND

www.ambassador-international.com

One Way to Grace:
A Memoir through Scripture

© 2013 by David Daly

All rights reserved.

ISBN: 978-1-62020-233-3 (paperback)
eISBN: 978-1-62020-331-6 (digital)

Unless otherwise indicated, Scripture taken from the King James Version of the Holy Bible. Public Domain.

Cover design and typesetting: Matthew Mulder
E-book conversion: Anna Riebe

AMBASSADOR INTERNATIONAL
Emerald House
427 Wade Hampton Blvd.
Greenville, SC 29609, USA
www.ambassador-international.com

AMBASSADOR BOOKS
The Mount
2 Woodstock Link
Belfast, BT6 8DD, Northern Ireland, UK
www.ambassadormedia.co.uk

The colophon is a trademark of Ambassador

Dedicated to our Lord and Savior Jesus Christ.
In memory of David's mother, Grace Smalley.

ACKNOWLEDGEMENTS

David thanks the divine guidance of Christ and the power of God for the opportunity to share his testimony with the world. The love of his late mother Grace and dear wife Gay resonate in David's heart, making the honesty and bravery of this work possible. David also thanks his dad, sister, brothers, son, grandson, and friends for being part of the memoir's creation. All glory to God.

Dawn would like to extend thanks to her husband Benjamin and mother-in-law April for their efforts and support. She also acknowledges the love, support, and patience of her friends and family throughout the writing process, on this and every piece she creates.

TABLE OF CONTENTS

CHAPTER ONE

Matthew 5:10–12 . . . . *9*

CHAPTER TWO

1 Corinthians 10:13 . . . . *15*

CHAPTER THREE

Romans 5:3–5 . . . . *25*

CHAPTER FOUR

Mark 10:6–9 . . . . *29*

CHAPTER FIVE

Ephesians 5:22–25 . . . . *35*

CHAPTER SIX

Mark 7:20–23 . . . . *41*

CHAPTER SEVEN

Proverbs 5:20–23 . . . . *51*

CHAPTER EIGHT

Psalms 34:17–20 . . . . *55*

CHAPTER NINE

1 Peter 5:8 . . . . *61*

CHAPTER TEN

1 Peter 4:12–13 . . . . *65*

CHAPTER ELEVEN

Ephesians 5:14–18 75

CHAPTER TWELVE

1 John 1:9 85

CHAPTER THIRTEEN

Mark 13:11 91

CHAPTER FOURTEEN

Jeremiah 1:19 97

CHAPTER FIFTEEN

2 Corinthians 4:8–9 103

CHAPTER SIXTEEN

1 Timothy 2:11–12 109

CHAPTER SEVENTEEN

1 Peter 5:10–11 117

CHAPTER EIGHTEEN

2 Corinthians 1:3–4 123

CHAPTER NINETEEN

Psalms 84:11–12 127

CHAPTER TWENTY

Romans 1:16–17 131

CHAPTER TWENTY-ONE

Psalms 100 137

CHAPTER ONE

*Blessed are they which are persecuted for righteousness' sake: for theirs is
the kingdom of heaven.*
*Blessed are ye, when men shall revile you, and persecute you, and shall say
all manner of evil against you falsely, for my sake.*
*Rejoice, and be exceeding glad: for great is your reward in heaven: for so per-
secuted they the prophets which were before you.*
MATTHEW 5:10–12

I HAD HEARD OF A place called Jerusalem, had read about
the Mount of Beatitudes, and had studied the Sea of Galilee.
My imagination had created the Israel depicted in the Bible. The
backdrop and scenery of these parables, lessons, and histories had
been developed by my mind and soul when I closed my eyes and
enveloped my thoughts in the Word.

To see that these places were real and exactly how my mind
had shaped them was overwhelming. Words I had studied so
closely were coming to life all around me. The stony ground
and squat olive trees of No Man's Land were there as I had
imagined. The gently sloping water of the Sea of Galilee was
the horizon ahead of me as it had been ahead of the disciples so
long ago. The wind brushing against my face swirled downward
from the same sky that hung over Christ as He traversed this
same body of water.

It was 2006 and I was in Israel for the second time, riding
a boat across the Sea of Galilee. All around me, the other passengers on the boat were rejoicing. They also knew the nature

of this trip. This water held the same meaning for them as for me; they too were celebrating the privilege to exist in this sacred place. To be physically present where our Savior had performed miracles, delivered sermons, and given his life was a blessing beyond any of our comprehensions.

The constant hum of the boat's motor melted into the sounds of worship, prayer, and joyous music. My eyes focused intently on the hills in the distance. There stood the Mount of Beatitudes. Jesus Christ himself had stood in that spot and ministered to expectant followers seeking guidance and a closer connection with God. The same guidance I sought a few short years before this trip, the same connection I still pursue each day.

As the realization of my close proximity to the Savior's ancient footprints began to overpower my composure, I felt a warm tingling sensation at the crown of my head. Unexpected and inexplicable, the feeling of pins and needles on my head became more intense. I closed my eyes and began to pray.

My prayers were those of thanks, gratitude, and reverence. I thanked God for leading me to this place, to where his Son had walked on water. As I prayed, the sounds of the boat, of the passengers' jubilation, the water, and the wind melted away, leaving me in a warm silence, alone with the tingling that was now so clearly the hand of God upon my head. For what seemed like eons, I stood on that boat with eyes closed, never wanting to open them and remove myself from this pure, unadulterated feeling of God's presence. I continued to pray for those I loved, for those who had hurt me, for all God's children, and all our souls. It was my only desire then to remain in that state for all time with my joy, my prayers, and my God's hand reaching down to touch me.

It was then that I learned what true beauty could be.

––––––––––––

I was born the eldest child of my parents, Clive and Grace, on May 28, 1965 at Dundonald Hospital in Belfast, Northern Ireland. A mere handful of years before what we call The

Troubles began to reach yet another violent climax.

I was brought into the world by a hardworking breadwinner and compassionate homemaker. We were a family of Protestants, Church of England and Church of Ireland respectively, living in the divided religious culture of Northern Ireland. There was a warzone hiding behind the façade of close-knit families, unlocked doors, and jubilant conversations over steaming cups of tea.

Through my child-sized eyes, Belfast was a gigantic living city, vivacious with noise and movement. Red brick buildings were adorned with full color murals declaring neighborhood allegiances. Haunting images of fallen heroes, hated figureheads, or gun-wielding gang members let those passing through know whether the inhabitants were loyal to the Union Jack or the Green White and Gold, to the Catholic or Protestant interests. By studying the painted curbs, proudly hung flags, or larger than life murals, you would know who was welcome and who was likely to be jumped in the streets or alleyways. A bustling capital rife with an underlying tension of religious unrest; the first memories I retain of my childhood were formed in Belfast.

My father and I walked toward my school on a clear, dry day in 1969.

I dreaded school.

The darker hue of my skin and the religious beliefs of my family separated me from most of my peers. Despite a ravenous appetite for learning and a small collection of friends, the idea of spending another day enduring the verbal—and sometimes physical—abuse of bullies tied my stomach in knots.

As my father and I reached the end of Shannon Street, I saw a dead dog lying in the street. A man, the dog's owner or perhaps a simple passerby, walked toward its crumpled and bloodied body. The man grabbed the dead dog by its tail. He dragged it to the gutter and out of the way of traffic. My four-year-old heart broke for that abandoned and mutilated dog.

A few months later, I nearly joined the ranks of that dog.

I had been tasked by my mother to walk to the store near

our home and purchase a bottle of brown sauce. With a bit of old money in hand and shopping list in mind, I ventured up the street on the short journey to the store. Across the road from me sat a happy little girl I did not recognize. She held the largest bag of crisps (potato chips) I had ever seen in her lap and was slowly eating as she sat on the front step of her home. When she saw me watching her, she met my eyes and lifted the giant bag of crisps as if to offer some to me. Excited, I changed course and started to run across the street.

A car I had not seen or heard approaching struck me as I crossed the road. When I came to, my father had me cradled in his arms, and he was running. As fast as he could force his legs to move, my father was carrying me to the hospital. I survived that close brush with death, the first of several I would encounter in my lifetime.

At the age of five, my family moved to the country, to Downpatrick. This relocation, twenty miles away from Belfast, represented a beacon of hopefulness and new beginnings. Perhaps, I thought, this new place would mark an end of the bullying and the start of a life without fear. What I did not understand was that The Troubles were not exclusive to imposing Belfast but were equally as prevalent, if not more pronounced, in rural Downpatrick.

When we first arrived in Downpatrick, our little family was without accommodation. At the time, two of my four younger siblings, Walter and Desmond, had been born. My granny, my mother's mother, welcomed the five of us into her home in the Meadowlands council housing estate. It took a year and a half for the county to assign us to our own council housing in the Flying Horse Estate.

The backdrop was eerily similar to what we had left behind in Belfast. The houses and curbs were marked with audacious symbols of devotion. While we children played mischievous games like Nick Knock, dodging burnt out cars as we ran away after knocking on strangers' doors, our fathers guarded our homes. The atmosphere living in the Flying Horse Estate housing was stiffened with the constant threat of danger. Our Protestant family was severely outnumbered, and there was a need for perpetual vigilance and awareness. My age did not make me exempt to the peril. Loyalty to cause, to family, and to religion extended to the younger generation; words and weapons hurt just as deeply in smaller, more fragile hands.

The bullying I experienced at Downpatrick Primary School was, if anything, more constant and aggressive than that which I went through in Belfast. There was no reprieve in the country; the fantasy of relaxing into a quiet existence in the country with a safe and calm family evaporated into a string of disconcerting experiences with my fellow children.

My own pride, even as a young person, did not allow me to break down but instead inspired me to stand tall and take the abuse, despite feeling broken and scared inside. The details are unclear in my memory due to the frequency of the harassment. One little girl remains vivid, however, as the personification of the persecution I experienced at that young age. Perhaps it was her fairer gender or the proximity of our homes but, for whatever reason, this girl's face, her voice, and more over her words ring clear in my mind decades later.

As if this vicious girl did not have enough ammunition from my familial fidelities, I was also of a darker complexion than the other children. I kept the sun; instead of the milky pallor of my classmates, my skin glowed a ruddy tan all year. My coloring led to cries of racist slurs like *nigger* being hurled in my direction as well as those related to my family and my inherited faithfulness to the Union Jack. From the perspective of the majority of my classmates, represented in my recollection by this single young girl, everything about me was wrong. Their voices rose in taunts that injured more seriously than the scraps and fights that came along with the hecklings.

CHAPTER TWO

*There hath no temptation taken you but such as is common to man: but
God is faithful, who will not suffer you to be
tempted above that ye are able; but will with the temptation also
make a way to escape, that ye may be able to bear it.*
1 CORINTHIANS 10:13

W HEN I WAS TEN, we made a move to council housing
on a street called Mount Crescent. Loyalist Protestant
families were present in greater numbers on Mount Crescent
and the neighboring Bridge Street. There was safety in numbers.
A row of houses filled with Loyalists could stand stronger than
one small family surrounded by those perceived as the enemy.
There was still the pressure of The Troubles, but it seemed less
daunting with like-minded families nearby.

The concentration of Protestant men, women, and children
on Mount Crescent and neighboring Bridge Street may have offered an intermittent sense of security, but it also made our new
estate housing a target for IRA and zealous Catholic attacks. As
a small boy of ten, I sat in our living room that overlooked all
of Downpatrick with my knees gathered to my chest, guarding
a milk crate of petrol bombs that could defend our home in
the worst-case scenario. My mother, cousins, and other family
members were gathered around me with functional weapons
like chains and bats. When the sun set, my father and other
brave male residents served as sentries at either end of the street,
hoping that the moment never came when their sons and wives

would need to hurl those bombs at snarling, screaming, violent people.

Most days the children were able to be children. Organizations like the Boys' Brigade—we called ourselves the Life Boys—gave us a sense of togetherness and purpose. The other boys and I put on our field caps and gathered at the parochial hall once a week, on Wednesdays, to learn how to be strong British men with knowledge of the outdoors, faith, and teamwork. That hall was a safe place for me, for a while.

The meetings would let out right at 8:30 p.m. every Wednesday evening. After the meeting was over, I would walk to my aunt's house, five hundred yards away, which was closer to the hall than my family home at the time. For reasons I cannot remember now, the other boys and I were let out fifteen minutes early one night and left the hall around 8:15 p.m. As I reached the gate to my aunt's front yard and placed my hand on the latch, the loudest sound I'd ever experienced resounded through the streets from the direction of where I had just been.

Someone with anti-imperialist motives had detonated a 500-pound bomb in the parochial hall. Why they targeted the children of those they were fighting against may never be fully understood. Had the Boys' Brigade gathering ended at the usual time, at 8:30 p.m., the entire troop would have been slaughtered. As it was, I was lucky to be far enough away from the explosion not to be killed or injured in the blast. Shop windows were blown out, car alarms were alerting, and the hall was devastated. A few minutes later, there was my father, once again rescuing me from a near death experience. He forced his way through the gathering police officers and emergency vehicles, risking an assault charge by pushing the police, to pick me up and bring me home. Together we thanked God for my early departure from the Boys' Brigade.

Religion and God were a casual part of my life since I was old enough to sit still and quietly listen. The memories of my childhood contain nothing of my parents joining us at church. I recall, however, admiring the way my dad read the family's copy of the Bible, marveling at his ability to find meaning and truth in ornate language I was still too young to comprehend. Our mother would quote Scripture while correcting behavior and lending advice, but neither of them ever joined us at worship. Yet, my brothers Walter, Desmond, and I attended Sunday school at a Baptist church faithfully every week. My parents obviously acknowledged the importance and impact of a child's early exposure to Christ's teachings and the community of believers churches represent. As I grew into my faith years later, I began to understand that their motivations to remove themselves from the organized churches were their own and did not detract from their belief and trust in God.

There were other children with us on those Sunday mornings, all absorbing God's Word in a way that was filled with light. We sang songs and learned the lessons and stories of the Bible. The church was small, and the schoolhouse where Sunday lessons were taught was even smaller. No more than seven to ten children could comfortably sit and learn from the teacher at one time. Had the church been larger or Sunday school more crowded, I—as a timid child—may have been too intimidated and shy to fully enjoy and absorb what was being spoken. Thankfully it was an intimate setting where I could relax and open my heart.

The Sunday school often organized outings for children. Wholesome, educational activities were sponsored, such as swimming and orienting. Bangor was a popular destination for these outings. Fifteen to twenty children would pile onto a small bus with one or two adult escorts and head out for the town of Bangor to go swimming.

On my first trip to Bangor, a few other children and I became separated from our chaperone. I was ten at the time and felt responsible for the younger children in my midst. The layout of the streets and the location of our intended destination were unknown to me. Yet, my instincts told me where to go. I led the other children with me as I navigated the streets. While I was aware of never having visited this town before, the correct path seemed so obvious, as if I were being led by a length of twine tied snugly to my soul. Eventually, my fellow lost children and I found the church hall where we were meant to be. My parents were later informed of my good deed and were adulated for making sure I was aware of my surroundings the last time we visited Bangor.

"We've never brought David to Bangor," my mother and father said. Their voices had sounded confused but proud.

The next time I visited Bangor, County Down, on a Sunday school trip, the events that occurred were less pleasant but no less blessed or touched by Christ. We had taken the bus to Bangor for the purpose of visiting the public swimming pool. I had never been to a pool and certainly had never learned how to swim. I was more curious than afraid. There was bound to be a lifeguard keeping an eye on the swimmers, and I had to be safe there if the Sunday school escorts were secure in bringing their young charges for a swim.

After changing out of my street clothes and into swimming trunks in the locker room, I walked down the damp concrete hallway toward the open area of the pool. The first thing I saw was a depth marker that let me know that the pool was three feet deep. What was left of my fear subsided when I assured myself that I could stand up in the three-foot pool and the water would be comfortably below the level of my mouth, nose, and eyes. I walked slowly but assuredly into the pool.

Because I had never been to a pool like this before, it at no point occurred to me that while where I stepped in was a mere three feet in depth, the far end that I was moving toward reached a maximum depth of sixteen feet. The floor of the pool steadily declined, causing the water level to rise subtly as I walked closer to the center. As the water reached my stomach and then chest, I felt my legs give way as my head quickly plunged beneath the surface. My arms flailed wildly and a muffled call for help sent bubbles cascading around my head. There was a steel bar along the edge of the pool, a safety measure for those unsure of their swimming ability. If I could reach it, I would be saved. I felt my muscles quickly weaken. My mind began to fade and darken. The moment I realized I could no longer fight to swim, an arm reached into the water and lifted me from the pool. The lifeguard who saved me from drowning made sure I was breathing and helped me calm down. Even though I survived my third near death experience, water terrified me for decades afterward. The sensation of my mind slipping away, my air being trapped inside my lungs, never left me completely.

At fifteen, a decade after I first started attending that Baptist Sunday school, I came home from church one Sunday and went into my bedroom alone. I had been learning about the journey of Jesus Christ and the persecution, abuse, and struggles He experienced before laying His life down for the sins of man. If He could rise above the torment and tyranny He endured on the cross, then perhaps welcoming Him into my heart could assist me and guide me to a calmer, more joyous existence.

There had been no prompting at Sunday school. No authority figure, teacher, or parent had instructed me to take part in this private moment with God. Inspired by the tribulations of Jesus and what His death and rebirth represented for all of mankind, I fell to my knees in my bedroom, as a fifteen-year-old boy, and brought my hands together in prayer. I thanked Jesus for His sacrifice and asked Him into my heart. By myself, with God and His Son, I relinquished control and surrendered, hoping for a peaceful future.

Two weeks later, temptation led me away from that peace and into a life of bondage that would extend for over twenty years.

My best mate, Gary, and I spent most evenings together playing, exploring, and generally being active young boys. One night while messing about the town, he and I went to the off-license store and purchased a twenty-four pack of Tennent's lager and a small bottle of Clan Dew wine blended whiskey. Beautiful, scantily clad pinup girls smiled at us from the sides of the Tennent's cans, inviting us with their coy smiles to drink up and join the fun.

We sat by the railway lines that ran by the technical college and opened our first cans from the case. After swallowing a few large and bitter gulps of the lager, we topped the cans off with short pours from the blended whiskey. The sugary wine and whiskey combination did nothing for the smell or taste of the alcohol in the cans.

After several more sips from our cans, we decided to go on a small adventure. Bravery, curiosity, and perhaps stupidity were encouraged by the potent alcohol now coursing through our veins. Gary and I walked the short distance to the technical college with lager cans and a brick or two shoved into our pockets. At that time, around 9:00 p.m., the college was empty and dark. No one was there to observe two young men shimmying up the drainpipes that ran up the side of the building. Gary grabbed his pipe, I grabbed mine, and together we scaled the building until we came to a window twenty feet from the ground.

A brick was put through the window, and we were inside. The classroom we entered was just as empty as the rest of the building, but teenage nerves combined with the beginning stages of drunkenness played tricks with my mind. Every rustle of wind outside or creak of settling floorboards was perceived as an approaching security guard, instructor, or police officer. As we threw chairs around the room, drank more lager, and wrote profanity on the chalkboard, Gary and I continually stopped and listened for the inevitable moment when we would be caught. That moment never came, and we managed to finish our mischief and escape unseen.

I have no recollection of climbing back down the drainpipe with Gary, hiding the rest of our liquor under a bush, or making my way home. I do remember the feeling of freedom, the lack of worry, and the irreverent—although manufactured—happiness that filled my body as I experienced alcohol for the first time. The door had been opened in my mind, and drinking was a part of my life. Pure and hopeful devotion to Christ was quickly replaced with the instant gratification of being drunk. The promises I made to God were pushed to the side as I surrendered instead to temptation.

Despite my newfound hobbies of drinking and gambling, school remained a priority and a source of pride. No amount of bullying or aggression could fully distract me from my studies. The only person able to pull my focus was an adult, a teacher with a malicious aggravation toward my family.

There were more than a dozen of my family members (me, my siblings, and cousins) who attended the school. For some reason this teacher, Mr. Rogers, had it in for my family. Whether it was the older cousins pushing his buttons or some other frustration he had toward us, his hatred vented toward the younger, more helpless family members—like me. This man was antagonistic, insufferable, and abusive. He posed a threat to my enjoyment of school with bullying that closely mirrored the jeers and harassment of the children.

Soon after Gary and I had our first experiment with alcohol, Mr. Rogers left the school. No one was sure where he had gone, maybe back to South Africa where he had come from or to some other far-flung destination, but it didn't matter much. He was gone, and I could relax back into my adoration of learning. I began to balance school work during the day with getting drunk and cutting loose at night. Fruit (slot) machines and lager became a part of my routine right beside textbooks and exams.

Soon it was time to further my education. While the big university in Belfast was out of the question due to the cost, if I lived to my apparent potential, I could go to the smaller school in Downpatrick and learn my trade. I had no inclination toward one career or another. The school called my parents in and told them of my skill for technical drawing. I was an architect in the making, they said, and should attend college. I chose to go to

Downpatrick Technical College to study technical drawing, to become something more.

I was over-the-moon. To become an architect would mean an easier existence. Hard work, perseverance, and a natural talent had paid off for me, it seemed, and my horizon appeared brighter. On my first day of classes at Downpatrick Technical College, I was anxious but assured. Technical drawing came easily to me, and success felt like a sure thing. My odds of doing well were better than those I played with on the fruit machines. I held my head high as I entered the room where my first class was held. It could have been the same classroom Gary and I had trashed several months before, but adolescent mischief was far from my thoughts at that moment.

Once inside the classroom, however, my high hopes fell to the floor. Mr. Rogers, the nightmare of a teacher from the secondary school, was standing at the front of the room. Like the punch-line of a dark joke, this hateful man was the instructor. The optimistic nervous energy I had been riding all morning turned to a nauseating dread. I fought the urge to simply turn around and walk back out, back home and away from my lofty plans of becoming an architect. Bravely, I walked to an empty desk.

As my knees bent to sit down, Mr. Rogers came quickly across the room and pulled the chair out from under me. My backside hit the floor hard. Embarrassment and concern for what would happen next brought a flush to my face as I tried to get up. Mr. Rogers grabbed me by the scruff of my neck and told me to stand outside the room. He followed me, and when the door closed behind us, he grabbed me by the neck. I was small for sixteen, thin and not very tall, and Mr. Rogers seemed a giant. His large hand closed around my throat, restricting my air, and he lifted me several inches off the ground. I was being strangled.

"You haven't got your family here now, have you?" he hissed angrily. There may have been more said but my fear of dying at the hands of my attacker blocked out any other sounds.

I wanted to fight back, to scream. More than that, though,

I wanted to go to class. The future I had begun to picture was so close. My fingertips were brushing against the edge of a new life in which I designed buildings and helped shape the skyline. When Mr. Rogers released my throat from his grasp, I was happy to breathe again but sadly knew there would be no college for me here. If, on the first day, I was being strangled, there was no telling what would happen after days, weeks, or months of being stuck in a room with that man.

Mr. Rogers told me to report to the headmaster's office; he would surely devise some offense to accuse me of, and I would be punished. Fear won out, ambition took a backseat, and I left. I never went back to college. I gave up on becoming an architect. I made up a series of excuses to my parents as to why I wasn't attending classes and found other ways to pass the time. If I had told my parents—especially my father—the truth, there would have been more trouble. I buried the fear, confusion, and disappointment deep inside.

Years passed before I was able to understand that the attack I endured from Mr. Rogers was not my fault. The hatred and anger he had was not a result of some wrongdoing on my part. Still, I carried the pain and humiliation of having college taken from me for a long time and, looking back, not taking advantage of my potential played a large role in how my early adult life took shape.

CHAPTER THREE

And not only so, but we glory in tribulations also:
knowing that tribulation worketh patience;
And patience, experience; and experience, hope:
And hope maketh not ashamed;
because the love of God is shed abroad in our hearts
by the Holy Ghost which is given unto us.
ROMANS 5:3–5

IN MY LATE TEENS, dancing was freedom. An intoxicating combination of pulsing beats, attractive women, and plenty of alcohol lit a fire inside my seventeen-year-old body. While moving to the music, I was able to escape the explosions, the gunshots, and the fear. A full-time job at a small hardware store put some extra money in my wallet to fund these adventures. The nightclub inside the Slieve Donard Hotel in Newcastle was my favorite place to go dancing. A beautiful hotel on the coast, the Slieve Donard was a mere thirteen miles away from where I lived with my family.

My cousin Robert and I hitchhiked to Newcastle on an idyllic summer night. The hours he and I spent dancing, drinking, and flirting with girls passed in a blur, as every night of partying does. We emerged into the early morning twilight, the sky still dark but threatening a sunrise. With the landscape that inspired the fictional land of Narnia hugging tightly against the shoreline, Robert and I began our journey home. The tourist town was quiet and nearly empty at two in the morning, a serene backdrop to the tingling afterglow of a night spent moving to the rhythms of nightclub music.

We could see a fire burning on the beach from where we walked. There must be girls there, he and I agreed, the kind of girls who leave a club at closing time with no intention of stopping their rowdy celebrations. The decision to break from the street and wander onto the sand toward the fire was an easy one to make. As we grew closer to the group gathered around the warming flames, however, the mistake we had made became evident. These were not our hoped-for party girls. Instead of beautiful women, Robert and I were walking toward a huddle of skinheads.

The handful of rough and tumble men spotted us a moment after my cousin and I realized our error, and they began to chase us. If we were caught by these skinheads, we surely would be beaten. Violence to these types was a game, and our younger, smaller bodies were easy fodder for their fun.

During the pursuit, I fell hard to the ground and tore the right knee of my trousers. In the scramble to regain my footing and continue to flee with Robert the wallet I kept tucked into my pocket was lost. I didn't notice at the time that it was gone but would know soon enough. As the distance between the skinheads and the two of us grew, we slowed our pace and tried to regain our breath. It was then that the absence of my wallet came to my attention, and I kept my eyes open for a police officer to whom I could report the loss. Not much time passed before a police car passed by, and I flagged it down. The officer inside took my information along with the story of the skinheads and dropped wallet. I made mental note of his officer number and we parted ways. Robert and I started back down the road toward home with thumbs extended, hoping for a ride to be offered by a kindly driver. We thought the worst of the night's events were done with, and we were ready to be safely in our homes, in our beds.

Several minutes later, as my cousin and I slowly walked toward home, another police car came to a stop across the road from us. The officer got out of the car and approached Robert and me.

"Which of you is Daly?" the officer called.

I thought he'd found my wallet or knew what had happened to it and could help me. I said I was Daly and started to walk toward him. Before I could fully process what was happening to me, the officer had me by the collar and was tossing me head first into the back of the police car.

What Robert and I hadn't realized was that the gang of skinheads who chased us from the beach had seen my dropped wallet and pocketed it. Then the motley criminals had committed a robbery at a nearby grocery store, leaving my wallet behind as a decoy. My torn pant leg became evidence of being at the scene of the robbery, not of falling down while being pursued by the real offenders. I was on the line for a crime I had nothing to do with or any knowledge of.

Once at the police station, Robert and I were placed in separate rooms. Investigators questioned me relentlessly. My assertions of the truth, that the wallet was planted at the store by the gang of skinheads and that my cousin and I had no part in the robbery, were ignored. Several of the investigators spoke at the same time, asking the same questions over and over. They were trying to catch me out, to confuse me into confessing to the robbery so their work could be done and the arrest made.

I remembered the badge number of the officer I had reported the lost wallet to and offered it as proof. Shortly after pleading my case and giving the officer's number, that same policeman came into the room. He looked me right in the eye.

"You reported a lost wallet to me?" his voice boomed over the cacophony of the station and the other investigators hushed. "You didn't report nothing to me."

I asserted yet again that I had reported my loss to him, that he must remember me.

"You calling me a liar?" he asked.

The anger coming off of him was terrifying. I could not understand why this officer of the law was entirely rejecting reality, tossing my words aside as lies so easily. At that he produced his rifle and swung it, hitting me in the face. I was knocked out cold on the floor of the interrogation room. My role in the conversation was over, and my fate was in the hands of my persecutors.

Through some kind of divine intervention, I was saved from wrongful arrest and prosecution by a family friend who happened to be a parole officer in the area. Word of my detainment and injury got to him, and he came to the station. Both Robert and I were let go without official charges being filed. I never fully trusted the police again. Our own lascivious desires had taken my cousin and me into a dangerous situation, but it was the antagonistic yet indifferent nature of the local authorities that escalated a close brush into a full-on collision with disaster. I walked away from the experience in a daze of confusion and disbelief. How could this have happened to a pair of innocent teenage boys?

A simple, lustful desire to dance and revel resulted in a disillusion of the safety leant to me by the presence of police officers. At any moment, I could be falsely accused, tossed in a police cruiser, and swept away from my entire life. My words, the truth, these things meant nothing if enough authority figures believed an easy lie. As an adult I understood that none of the trouble in Newcastle would have happened if I hadn't been tempted toward the sparkling lights and bumping beats of the Slieve Donard nightclub. We, Robert and I, had opened the door to those consequences ourselves. My teenaged perception, however, just saw the unfair treatment and painful blow to the head as something else to escape, to drink away, and to blame.

CHAPTER FOUR

But from the beginning of the creation God made them male and female.
For this cause shall a man leave his father and mother,
and cleave to his wife; And they twain shall be one flesh: so then
they are no more twain, but one flesh. What therefore God hath joined to-
gether, let not man put asunder
MARK 10:6–9

MORE THAN A YEAR after my traumatic experience in Newcastle, I was still working at the hardware store, still experimenting with alcohol, gambling, and nightclubs. Every morning I would run from my home in Mt. Crescent to the store a quarter of a mile away. On my route to work, I would pass the bus stop outside of the Downpatrick Town Hall as the bus was getting ready to depart with its passengers.

One morning I happened to glance at the bus as I hurried past the Town Hall. Two girls were looking out the window and smiling at me. It was a bright morning, and soft rays of sunlight reflected off the metal and glass of the bus. One of the girls caught my eye, and I was struck with anxious happiness by how beautiful the girl smiling at me was, morning sunlight wrapped around her gentle face. I made eye contact with her but continued on my way without pausing. There was work to get to, and the moment of recognition had flushed my cheeks with instinctual embarrassment.

For the next several mornings, I made sure I looked a little tidier, a little more impressive for my run past the Town Hall. I tried my best to time my commute so I could pass the bus right as it was arriving. On mornings when I arrived at the stop before the bus, I would hang back and wait for it. The stunning young girl and her friend continued to peer out of the bus window at me as I ran. My heart skipped and leapt with every step toward where I knew my mystery girl sat on the bus with her mate. A month or so into this silent acknowledgement, smiling at one another through a window, the girls starting opening the glass flap and calling out to me in a pair of giggling, lilting voices. A shy and timid nature kept both her and me from speaking to one another directly, though. Personally, I had very limited one-on-one experience interacting with pretty girls unless it was in the uninhibited atmosphere of a pub or nightclub. I was unsure of how to sound cool and collected around a creature who made me nearly shake with nervousness. With a sober mind in the clear light of day, the confidence I had at the bars vanished.

After three or four months of exchanging warm looks and smiles, the object of my adoration's bolder friend made the first contact. This brassy girl, whose name turned out to be Maggie, hopped off the bus as I ran past and got my attention.

Her friend Cathy fancied me, she said. They were going out to the Millbrook Lodge in Ballynahinch, County Down. She invited me to join her and Catherine on the stipulation that I had to bring a male mate of mine for Maggie. Without hesitation, I accepted the offer and agreed to meet Maggie and Catherine at Millbrook Lodge for a double date.

My good mate Phillip was easy to convince. After describing the outgoing and pretty nature of his unexpected date, Maggie, and expressing my utter need to know the one called Catherine, he agreed that our Saturday night venture would be the double date with the girls from the bus. We knew of Millbrook Lodge, had enjoyed a drink or two there in the past. Even if the double date turned into a disaster, I knew I would end up having a good time with Phillip.

That Saturday night, Phillip and I arrived at Millbrook Lodge in Ballynahinch before Maggie and Catherine. We drove my father's Austin Allegro out to the lodge. Even though I knew we would be drinking, I was not worried about driving the car home under the influence. Despite my harrowing experience just a year prior that involved the police, Phillip and I took the chance at being pulled over. There's a certain thrill to being a teenager, a sense of serene immunity. No amount of hardship could keep me from my decadent fun; I was seventeen and invincible.

We arrived shortly before the girls and had a chance to settle in and try to look cool for our dates' entrance. Even though Maggie entered the lodge before her, it was Catherine that caught my eye first. When I saw the beautiful blonde I would be spending my evening escorting, my heart nearly stopped. From her seat on the bus where we first encountered one another, all I had seen was her stunning face and shimmering hair. The limited view I had been able to get had left me unprepared for all that was Catherine. Her impossibly long and slender legs were encased in the tightest jeans I'd ever seen. Even with the shy smile curving her lips and the flicker of nervousness in her eyes, those legs spoke pure confidence.

Maggie did the talking when she and Catherine, whom she referred to as Cathy, reached me and Phillip. We decided to meet up in a few minutes so the girls could freshen up and say hello to friends of theirs. We would share a drink, maybe a few dances. I later learned that during this short initial conversation, my mate became immediately smitten with brazen Maggie and, of course, Cathy struck my fancy long before I saw her slink into Millbrook Lodge. It was shaping up to be a successful evening.

Whether it was due to the alcohol or the tingling elation of a new lustful attraction, the rest of the evening passed in a blur. I remember very clearly, however, the feeling of sureness and rightness that grabbed at my heart whenever I touched Cathy, whenever her eyes met mine. It was as if the world spun backward when she looked at me, slowing time to a crawl.

A stolen kiss or suggestively wandering hand on a dance floor was the long and short of my romantic endeavors. This lack of experience coupled with the deepness of what I already felt for this almost-stranger doubled my nervous energy and desire for just one more pint, one more shot. With the courage leant to me by the alcohol, I was able to court the intoxicating Cathy and left the bar that night with her on my arm.

The relationship developed quicker than either of us could have predicted. What started as a physical attraction and fascination evolved into a heartfelt new love. Within weeks we were inseparable, spending as much of our free time together as possible. Shortly after we took our courtship to a more intimate, physical level, things got even more serious.

Cathy and I were pregnant.

It was a foregone conclusion that I would make an honest woman out of my young love. There was only one acceptable response to conceiving a child with a girlfriend, and that response was marriage. At barely eighteen years old, I was preparing to become a father and a husband, but there was no regret in my heart. I loved Cathy, and she loved me; this could be the purpose and direction I had been lacking since leaving that technical drawing class just two years before. My mind turned to finding a ring, proposing to my future wife, and planning our life together.

Before I had a chance to put my plan into effect, Cathy and I went to visit with her family. My heart dropped when it was announced by Cathy's mother that the wedding album had been ordered and a ceremony date set. All wedding related decisions were jerked away from me as though my opinions, my thoughts were secondary to those of Cathy's female family members. Perhaps it was my immaturity, but I was overcome by a sense of unfairness, of being out of control of my own life. I had wanted to give Cathy a love story, a romantic moment she could show off. Instead, I was just another detail in a story I did not create.

The ceremony took place at the Downpatrick Church of Ireland on a warm and sunny April morning. Cathy was about five months pregnant, a lovely vision in her white dress with a curve of billowing volume added to her naturally slender frame.

She walked down the aisle toward me and our respective family members who stood on either side of the marriage altar. The bouquet she held against her midsection, a cascade of purple and pink blooms, would hide her half-term pregnancy in the photos, but the glow of an expectant mother still twinkled on her face.

The vows were simple, but I meant each word with every ounce of sincerity in my heart. My brother Walter stood by me as my best man, lending me his support. As I looked at my Catherine, my new wife carrying my new child, I felt safe in my love for her. I could imagine our life together, humble but happy in the small council housing we would eventually procure for the baby and us, as husband and wife. In the minutes it took to complete the marriage ceremony, I became steadfast in my belief that standing with Cathy reciting those promises was exactly where I was meant to be.

The reception was held afterward at a hotel in Cathy's home-town of Crossgar. The Hunters Moon was a small but inviting space that easily held our gathered friends and family. We sat at the head table, Cathy and I, with Walter to my right and Cathy's sister to hers. I remember our single tier wedding cake that remained in front of us throughout most of the reception. Its topper sparkled softly, as did the tiara pinned to the top of Cathy's dark blonde hair.

Overall, it was a beautiful day. The doubts anchored to the lack of control I had over the proposal and subsequent wedding retreated to the darkest depths of my thoughts as I slid the wedding band onto Cathy's finger. By the time we kissed and walked back down the aisle together, I was calm and comfortable on the path the unexpected pregnancy had chosen for me.

After a short honeymoon in Newcastle and before being granted council housing, Cathy and I moved into the spare room of my family home in Mt. Crescent. While awaiting the rapidly approaching birth of our baby, my new wife and I adjusted to our new roles as husband and wife. Even though the basement bedroom and bath provided little in the way of true privacy, the communal living situation allowed much needed practice for our new life as spouses and parents.

Our son was born a few months later in September. I named him Gary, after my dearest childhood friend. He was so small, so fragile. I felt just as fragile as I held him for the first time. The love I immediately felt for this miniature version of Cathy and I overwhelmed my heart. Romantic love is emboldening, a strengthening and invincible feeling. The love one feels for a child, though, is much different. To know that this unmarred, unhurt, untouched soul is in your charge is all at once exhilarating and terrifying. I could barely care for myself; how could God expect me to take on the wellbeing of a wife and newborn son? Yet, there he was. Gary Daly, my son, swaddled in a blanket and sleeping soundly in my arms. Part of me will always see him that way, as the best of me wrapped in plush poly-cotton blend.

CHAPTER FIVE

Wives, submit yourselves unto your own husbands, as unto the Lord.
For the husband is the head of the wife, even as Christ is the head of the
church: and he is the saviour of the body. Therefore as the church is subject
unto Christ, so let the wives be to their own husbands in every thing.
Husbands, love your wives, even as Christ also loved the church,
and gave himself for it;
EPHESIANS 5:22–25

CATHY, BABY GARY, AND I moved into our council housing on Bridge Street. The house that would be our first home had previously belonged to an aunt and uncle of mine, Mary and Nathaniel. I was happy to have the familiarity with our living space and knew Cathy and I could make it our own, filling the rooms with our own happy family memories.

I had a job at the hardware store and a part-time commitment to the Territorial Army to bring financial support to our little household. While I was still drinking in what little free time I had to spare, the largest part of my efforts went toward being the kind of husband and father I felt Cathy and Gary deserved—the best. Of course, two new parents barely out of their teens felt a fair amount of pressure to succeed and prosper. We knew what functional husbands and wives looked and sounded like; we formed our actions to that ideal. What we did not understand, could not understand at that point in our naïve lives, was that work and struggle went into that ideal family. You cannot take a young woman and force her into the mold of doting wife and mother, just as you cannot transform a drunken party boy into the perfect head of household overnight. Not without some squalling and pain, that is.

The neighbors loved us. From the outside looking in, Cathy and I had a lovely marriage, an adorable child, and the perfect life. At my young age, I had everything. Most men work their entire lives trying to secure a good job, adoring wife, and bouncing baby to carry on the family name. Every want I'd ever had for stability, for love, and for purpose was becoming real.

Arguments broke out between Cathy and me on a regular basis and over the most trivial problems. The issues and disagreements that some couples take years of togetherness to avoid rose to the surface of our quickened marriage. One night as my wife and I blustered at one another over something so small and meaningless I forgot what it was minutes into the fight, Cathy picked up a jar of Sudocrem meant for Gary's nappy-covered bottom and chucked it directly at my head. If I had been as drunk as I had wished I was, my reflexes wouldn't have been sharp enough to avoid the ointment, and it would have struck me squarely in the forehead. My wife had one powerful arm and fine aim.

Instead of hitting its intended target, my head, and knocking me unconscious, the Sudocrem missed me by less than an inch and exploded all over the beautiful brown velvet curtains that guarded the privacy of our living room. Those curtains were some of the nicest possessions we had, and a frivolous disagreement between overwhelmed spouses ruined them.

On a cold night, there was a knock at the door. When I answered the knock and saw my father standing on my doorstep, I knew this was not a simple pop-in visit. With little grandness, he let me know that he and my mother were leaving Northern Ireland. As a native Englishman, a Protestant, and a soldier in the British army, my father was a perpetual target for violent attacks from those associated with the IRA and other impassioned guerrilla groups. I understood this danger all too well. I had experienced the paranoia of a soldier first hand while serving with the Territorial Army, checking under my car for bombs and changing routes to the camp every week. Every member of our family, those sharing our name and reputation, were equally as vulnerable. It was time for the Daly brood to leave the instability and danger of Northern Ireland for the safer shores of England, where my grandparents lived. He said it would be a good idea for me, as the man of my house, to gather up my wife, child, and essential belongings to follow them to England. To go anywhere. The important part was that I, and those I love, flee from danger. His face was stern, his voice stony. I knew he was deadly serious.

That's how Cathy, little baby Gary, and I wound up leaving our home. The relocation to England was not possible for us at that time, but the move to where her parents lived in Crossgar would keep us safe enough. We left everything we couldn't carry: clothing, silverware, furniture, and hundreds of other small items that don't seem important until you need to abandon them behind you.

My mother-in-law and I never got along. I could speculate about the reason behind our mutual dislike: her heavy-handed influence in Cathy's life or my perceived defilement of her precious daughter. No amount of explanation or understanding can go back and change the underlying pressure that lurked between Cathy's mother and me, though.

That small tension leached closer to the surface when my little family moved in with my in-laws. The sudden evacuation of our new house and departure of my parents for England had left us with precious few viable lodging options. Cathy's parents in Crossgar were the only sensible choice when we needed a place to land. So recently had I started getting used to my station as man of the house. Now, I was living under someone else's roof because choice was taken from me. Choice and free will, these are gifts. As easily as a gift is given, it can be taken away or lost. A young man has a hard time accepting new responsibility but an even rougher time losing it. In my mind, increasingly fueled by alcohol, I was being treated like a child when I had earned the right to be respected as a man.

It was clear that there wasn't enough room in Cathy's parents' house for all of us—me, Cathy, Gary, and my resentments. We moved into a small apartment over a shop Cathy's mother owned. From the window of the apartment, I could see the Hunter's Moon where my wife and I had celebrated our wedding reception. Maybe with the constant reminder of that happy day, I thought, I could get past whatever it was that tied my insides in knots only lager could untie. I saw the Hunter's Moon every day leaving for work. There it was when I returned home from the pub. During the arguments Cathy and I stumbled into, my eyes would glance out the window and, there it was.

It never got easier, though. My heart felt out of place without my family close at hand. My mother, father, and siblings were so ingrained in me; we are Our. More than a few dozen miles between them and me felt like the entire world. The knots became tauter every time I thought of it. The night the knots finally wound to their fraying point, the three of us were spending time at Cathy's parents' house. On that particular evening, I wanted to be anywhere but there. Anywhere as long as there was alcohol and not my in-laws. Once I felt as though I had fulfilled my obligation to this new family of mine, I was ready to leave. Cathy and the baby could manage the short walk back to the apartment. No harm, no foul.

That is not how Cathy or any of my in-laws saw the situation. An argument I had not expected—and did not understand the source of—began suddenly. They saw an irresponsible and impetuous young man. A man trying to walk away from his wife and child so he could go get drunk, go have fun. I wish I could have expressed to the angry, screaming woman my wife turned into that there was no fun happening at those bars. Sure,

I was smiling, laughing, and dancing with acquaintances, well-wishers, and the occasional friend. Beneath that lighthearted behavior was inky black resentment, growing and rising, tangling those knots tighter.

I tried to leave, and Cathy blocked my path. She was easy to get around, and so was her sister, who also chose to stand in my way. When Cathy called her brother over, I became concerned this quarrel would continue to escalate. My hands had stayed obediently by my sides when the two small women tried to pen me in at the landing of the stairs ahead of the front door. I could not guarantee continued self-control once the brother backed me into a corner or laid a hand on me in restraint. Cathy's brother came down the stairs to the front door to serve as a human roadblock. Of course, he put his hands on me to hold me in that house and, of course, I broke free and stormed out of the house. I had to get away from those people, including Mrs. Cathy Daly.

It was bitterly cold, dark, and snowing. The world was a harsh pattern of black and white. The snow fell all around me, and at first I wasn't sure exactly where I was going. To England, ultimately, I assumed. Though, I couldn't get there on foot. If I could have, I would have walked every inch that lay between me and my mother's kind, loving eyes. There would be swimming involved in that journey, though, and you couldn't catch me ankle deep in the Irish Sea. I still had an aunt in Antrim. That's where I could go and know I'd be let in from the cold. Aunt Ellen would surely open her home to a frozen and heartbroken nephew.

Roughly thirty miles was the distance between my in-laws in Crossgar and Aunt Ellen's in Antrim. Every footfall felt like twenty, and by the end of my trek, I would have sworn the ground I'd covered was closer to eighty or a hundred miles. I tried to hitch rides but, in the poor weather conditions, they were difficult to find. With stubbornness and pride, I trudged forward and thought. The well-paying government job I had just started before moving to Crossgar was gone. I had walked away from innocent baby Gary. My wife was fuming. What a mighty mess I had created.

Aunt Ellen welcomed me in from the snowy night, just as I had expected. Her house was bustling with her family, but loneliness permeated everything around me. While staying with my extended family, I tried repeatedly to make amends with Cathy. I threatened to go to England, and she told me to leave. There was so much acrimony between us that our relationship felt unfixable. Pride and stubbornness kept us puff-chested and steadfast. I would go to England, be with my family, and give my wife and I time to cool off so we could resolve this and be loving, functional parents.

CHAPTER SIX

And he said, That which cometh out of the man, that defileth the man.
For from within, out of the heart of men, proceed
evil thoughts, adulteries, fornications, murders,
Thefts, covetousness, wickedness, deceit, lasciviousness,
an evil eye, blasphemy, pride, foolishness:
All these evil things come from within, and defile the man.
MARK 7:20–23

ON JULY 23, 1985, I flew from Belfast to London. My parents had a small home in a village called Chilcompton. That was where I was going to stay until I found work and saved enough money to secure a new home for my family. I could send for Cathy and Gary, who would happily join me once everything was lined up and ready to go. What I did not plan on, however, was the effect leaving my wife and child behind would have on me. I could never have anticipated the intense sensation of emptiness that washed over me every day I woke up without them. I loved Cathy, and Gary was a living, breathing part of me. I knew I was capable of living without them. I was not so convinced that life would be anything you could call worthwhile, though.

I spent most days curled into a ball on the bed my parents had provided for me. Nights were spent at the pubs using the small unemployment benefits I received. I would stumble to bed after drinking away the uneasy pangs of loss I felt for my son and wife. This pattern continued for weeks with little variance.

While my father worked tirelessly to support my mother, me, and my siblings, I languished in the growing fear that the things I had so recently been given were never coming back to me. That fear fed the drunkenness that inevitably landed me in serious trouble.

The walk home from Redan Pub took me across a field. One evening, I had more to drink than usual and wandered aimlessly across the field, trying my best to find the house. In a fog of alcohol, I approached a window on the side of a house that was not my parents.' With house key in hand, I tried to unlock the window as if it were the front door. The resident of this strange house had seen my approach and came to the window I was trying to unlock. His appearance startled me, and I ran away, realizing my senseless mistake. The police had already been called, though, and the damage was done. I was charged with burglary with the intent to steal. There was nothing I could say to justify what I had done, and I paid my fine with little protest. I could see it on the face of my mother and father that, even though I had had no intention of stealing from that man's house, I had stolen something from them. A little bit of their respect for me was gone, and I had stolen it away.

Cathy and I spoke as often as I could. She wavered between frustrated indifference toward me and a weak agreement to join me in England. I tried to hide my brokenness, tried to make her believe we could be happy together in Chilcompton. It would be better here, I told her, less fighting and less struggle. Hearing her voice was a wonderful reprieve that did little to quell the depression that had taken over my waking thoughts. I sent what little money I could back to Northern Ireland to aid in the support of my son, anything to give Cathy the impression that our life here could work. My mind, body, and soul ached for the presence of her and my precious son. At the same time, the idea of introducing the tumultuous relationship Cathy and I had back into my everyday life was an elusively troubling concept.

It became obvious to my parents that Redan Pub was my only real reason to get out of bed. My lack of interest in finding reliable work was becoming more noticeable. After Cathy sent me half of the money for our old council housing furniture and most of that windfall was spent on liquor, it seemed as though my hardworking father had tired of my insolence.

He came into the bedroom where I was lying down. I barely responded to his entrance, which pushed his anger further. Before I could be fully aware of what was happening, my father grabbed the edge of my bed in both his hands, and I slid to the floor. Not only was he tossing me out of bed, but he was throwing me out of his home. He had grown tired of my melancholic sloth and thought a swift kick in the backside would incite some kind of responsible action. Perhaps I would return to Northern Ireland where my wife and child were, or maybe I would find work to bring in the money needed to bring my beloved Cathy and Gary to England.

Neither of those two outcomes happened. Instead, I retreated to Wookey Hole in Somerset, England, where my grandmother, called Nanny, and stepgrandfather lived. Wookey Hole was even less populated than Chilcompton, consisting primarily of caves, a pub, a small rank of houses, and one shop. Nanny's home was less than ten miles away, and after making my short trudge, the woman I always thought of as "good as gold" lovingly took me in. While I was happy to have the place to lay my head, it was a big adjustment to live with elderly family members. The transition was somewhat challenging. She and my granddad went to bed around seven in the evening. I would put on to them that I was retiring for the night as well and then sneak out shortly after they had fallen asleep. I was a grown man with a wife and child, tiptoeing out of my grandparents' house. I could have simply left: opened the front door and gone to the pub. Not wanting to call attention to my nightly excursions, I chose to creep around and lie. I knew that spending that much of my energy on drinking was unacceptable, deep down. Both Nanny and her husband must have been aware that I was up to something, but I let myself believe I was getting away with it.

Not long after I moved in with my grandparents, I discovered the jars.

Every year my Nanny and her husband would visit our family in Northern Ireland. While she was there, she would purchase generous gifts like appliances and clothing. What I never knew as a child and was very interested in finding out—as alcohol began to control more of my decision-making—was where the money for those gifts came from. All year, Nanny would tuck away a little money at a time in jars under the bed in the guest bedroom—my bed. It didn't take long for me to figure out what was stored beneath my sleeping head. Slowly, I began to siphon off the funds that had been so carefully tucked away. A little from this jar one night, more from another jar the next; I knew there was no way my grandparents would stay ignorant to my theft, but they would be oblivious to it long enough. Long enough for me to find a job, to begin replacing the money. Maybe Nanny would never notice the missing money if I could take small enough amounts, evenly distributed among the several jars, and begin repaying it soon.

It's amazing what you can force yourself to believe in order to justify terrible behavior.

After thirty-three unsuccessful job interviews, it became clear that my plan of putting back the stolen money was not going to pan out. My lack of reliable transportation and darkened demeanor made me an unattractive candidate for employment. This inability to find a job forced me to leave the stolen money stolen and, worse still, steal more. I was sure that getting caught and thrown back out on the street was inevitable.

The missing money was eventually noticed, but Nanny didn't ask me to leave. Perhaps her leniency had something to do with her experience with drinkers. My stepgranddad enjoyed hard cider much more than the average man. It could be that she understood what had driven me to steal from family, and she felt sorry for my state. I promised to find a job soon and replace the money, to avoid stealing more.

I managed to find a job working with ornamental pots in Wells at Redwoods Ornamental Stones. The owner was a patient and understanding older man who was willing to take a chance on me. I was grateful. On a weekly basis, I sent £10 postal orders to Cathy to help with Gary's care. This made me feel like a functional father and husband, no matter how distant. Most of the money I earned still went to nights out at the pub.

There was a man at the pub in Wells where I spent my money who had developed an aggressive dislike for me. At first, it was my Northern Irish accent that set him off. My bold and confident outward persona only goaded him further. This large, angry man frequently taunted me while I was at the pub. The voices of bullying classmates from my childhood echoed behind his in my mind, and one night I decided to put a stop to it. Even though he was substantially bigger than I was, I got it in my head that I could put him on the ground with a well-placed kick to the chest.

I got a running start and leaped into the air toward the man. Alcohol had given me the motivation to try this unusual attack but had given me no idea how to land after planting the kick in my opponent's chest. My feet hit the intended target, but the man did not fall. As I flew backward, I realized my lack of forethought and scrambled to get my legs back underneath me safely. I was once more unsuccessful and landed squarely on my back. The sidewalk was hard and unforgiving, and so was the man I had kicked. He grabbed me roughly and slammed my head into a concrete garbage bin near where I had landed. At first there was no pain, just a vibration thrumming through my head. I staggered to a standing position and did my best to run away from the violence I had started. As fast as I could manage, I rode my recently purchased motorbike back to my grandparents' house.

I did not know I was bleeding from the head when I went to bed fully dressed. The next morning, I awoke to a horrific amount of blood slowly drying on the pillowcase and bedclothes surrounding me. Nanny screamed when she saw the bed after

I had gotten up to wash and check my wounds. She and I both privately thanked God I hadn't died in my sleep from blood loss or a concussion. My gratefulness did not last long, however, and I was soon back at that same pub getting drunk.

Not only was I able to work and earn my keep, I was also able to meet people my own age while on the job. Reliably, I showed up for my shifts and behaved myself. Then, after work and on the weekends, my new mates and I would hit the pubs. My drinking had structure, and I felt in control of it. A functioning employee with healthy social ties does not have a problem with alcohol. It was impossible. My sense of control and functionality was strengthened when my employer came to the workroom looking for a lorry driver. I was the first to step forward and volunteer for the new position. My boss offered to pay for the HGV license, and I soon found myself delivering the ornamental pots instead of making them. This small success made me feel as though I had stepped onto the right path, after all.

After a while of making my own money and purchasing a vehicle, it was time to move out of my grandparents' house. The independence of working and socializing was driving me to find a more private living situation. Through an advertisement in the local newspaper, I found a woman who had a room to rent. The home on Churchill Road was close to my job, and I would have my own room, access to the kitchen, and plenty of privacy.

My conservative landlord had a usual habit of drinking a bottle of red wine with her evening meals. This practice of hers meant there was usually a good store of decent wine around the house. When my landlord wasn't paying attention, I would sneak quick swigs from an open bottle. Sometimes she would leave for a couple of weeks at a time to visit family in Spain. When those times came, I took it as an invitation to drink her wine and have parties in her home. A stream of women and friends would filter through the home, helping themselves to the wine as well as anything else they found around the house. I'm not sure why she put up with my disrespect for as long as she did; perhaps she needed the rent I paid her more than she missed the wine.

My choices outside of the house weren't any better. I had developed a friendship with Andy, a tall and thin hardworking man with partying habits similar to mine. He and I went down to Pretty Pond one evening to cut loose. I was driving the motorbike I had bought. During the work week, I drove a huge, heavy truck, and it was nice to zip around the countryside, open and free on my light motorbike.

As we approached the water, something in me lost control. Instead of parking my bike safely and jumping into the cool refreshing water or simply sitting next to it, I drove straight into Pretty Pond. I hit the water and lost my left shoe on impact. Though I managed to make it to shore and fish out my bike, the ordeal exhausted me. Eyes closed and chest heaving in labored breaths, I sprawled on the damp grass. My clothes were soaked and clinging to my chilled skin in weighty folds. As I drifted into an adrenaline and alcohol blackout, I remembered there was likely an adder or two slinking near me and I shouldn't let myself fall asleep.

In the morning when I woke up, slightly drier but freezing cold, I put my brain to work figuring out how to get back from the pond. Andy was gone. I still don't know when he left or if he thought I was dead when he did. Without a left shoe, I couldn't drive my motorbike. In a moment of simplistic genius, I crammed my right shoe onto my left foot and started the bike's engine. To this day, I'm amazed it started up as easily as it did.

The taillight was the only serious casualty of the pond. It kept going out, and I was concerned I would get pulled over. I couldn't afford a ticket and would most certainly be arrested for driving while intoxicated. While driving back to the old woman's house, my attention kept turning to the faltering taillight behind me. As I crested a famously steep hill in Wells, I turned back once more. That was one time too many, and I hit a curb at full speed. I was tossed off the bike and slid backward across the pavement. My leather jacket and helmet protected my head and torso, but my legs and hands were torn and bloodied. Two incredibly close calls with serious injury in a handful of hours, and still my first thoughts were on how good a drink would feel.

My job delivering the ornamental pots took me all over England, Scotland, and Wales. I would spend days on end traveling, staying in inexpensive bed and breakfasts, and collecting women in every city I frequented. Harrogate was a high class town populated by business people, doctors, and other upper crust success stories. My delivery partner and I decided to enjoy a night of dancing and lager at the local Soapbox Bar.

While standing at the bar slowly working on a pint and taking in the views, two women entered the bar. The woman at the front was stocky and sullen, but her friend following behind was stunning. In an experience similar to the first time I saw my wife Cathy, everyone else in the bar ceased to exist when I saw the tall, blonde, slender stranger join her friend at the edge of the dance floor. It wasn't until the undulating crowd of patrons parted for the women to pass that I remembered they were there. To my chagrin, the sea of people was not making a path for the model-esque woman, but for her companion instead. I cringed and quickly turned my back to her approach. She didn't take the hint offered by my abrupt change in body language and tapped me on the shoulder. I turned, mentally preparing her rejection to be as nice but concise as possible. Before I could say a word, she leant in and said, "My friend wants to see you."

I followed the larger woman out the door to a limousine parked outside. The beautiful blonde was sprawled in the back seat, beckoning me with a playful smile. My upbringing made me immediately suspicious of strangers luring me into cars at night. This kind of scenario usually ended up with a beating being given in an ally, or worse, where I was from. My libido and intoxicated judgment conspired against me, and I shook my misgivings away. After daring to get into this unknown woman's limo, I found out that she worked as a nurse and that her name was Cathy. A stone fell inside of me, knocking me off guard for a moment. This, too, I cast aside in exchange for whatever new Cathy's wily eyes had in store for me.

She took me to her lavish apartment in a gated complex nearby. Once inside, I was struck speechless by the luxury surrounding me. A double bed covered in wooly sheepskin, complex stereo speakers and a glorious bar held my attention for several minutes while we got comfortable. Nurse Cathy told me to help myself to a drink, which I did more than once. I spent the night with her. Not once during that night with Nurse Cathy did I think of my far away family, absentee fatherhood, or any other bleak realities.

The combination of alcohol and women finally relieved me of the nagging depression of my failing marriage. In the moments of drunkenness and pleasure, the trueness of my situation simply melted away, and what I could not fix, I was able to briefly forget.

CHAPTER SEVEN

And why wilt thou, my son, be ravished with a strange woman,
and embrace the bosom of a stranger?
For the ways of man are before the eyes of the Lord,
and he pondereth all his goings.
His own iniquities shall take the wicked himself,
and he shall be holden with the cords of his sins.
He shall die without instruction; and in the greatness of his
folly he shall go astray.
PROVERBS 5:20–23

MY FATHER HAD PROMISED my mother to return our family to Northern Ireland after two years if they were unable to find happiness in England. While England had been my father's home and he easily relaxed into life there, my mother missed Northern Ireland. As the two year deadline approached, tension began to creep into my family.

The delivery job that took me all over the country kept me away from the arguments and uncertainty. My brother Walter, however, had a front row seat to the problems. Walter lived in the same housing estate as my parents, and when an argument forced my father to leave their home for several hours, it was to Walter's home he went. He heard firsthand about my mother's increased drinking and how that did little to bring my father closer to her. She was lonely and could feel her husband pulling away from the marriage.

In hindsight, it would have been best for everyone if the

two of them had sat down and discussed what they were feeling. Those kinds of talks weren't the way families worked then, though. The man stoically absorbed his emotion, while the woman found slow, passive ways to express them. For my mother, that passive escape appeared in lager cans hidden around the home. Her growing dependency on alcohol fueled the anger, sadness, and loneliness. There were also troubling suspicions growing in her mind about my father's faithfulness.

Late nights at work became more frequent and less believable. Combined with his general indifference to her, his absences made my mother certain the love of her life was slipping away. My father, on the other hand, had watched the spark drain from his wife. The move to a new country had been rough on everyone but had been necessary for our safety and ability to thrive. In my father's eyes, Northern Ireland was a dangerous place to live, and by removing us from the uncertain situation, he was offering us new opportunities. He did not realize that uprooting his family for the promise of a better life would dismantle the marriage that held that family together.

Then, he met someone who could understand his frustrations and provide some comfort and distraction. A married woman who worked at the same alcohol bottling factory was having troubles with her spouse, as well. There was a mutual attraction from the start. I can only imagine how harmless flirtation and supportive listening transformed into a romantic attachment neither expected. Cliché wisdom teaches you cannot choose who you fall in love with. That may be true, but what you can choose is how you deal with falling. Later, after the dust had settled, my father told me it was possible to be in love with two women. That was the long and short of the explanation he offered for his infidelity. His heart was caught between two places.

Two decades of marriage make you acutely sensitive to your partner's moods and disposition. As soon as a portion of my father's affection was given to another woman, something in my mother's heart took notice. More cans of lager appeared around the house, both hidden and openly visible. Occasional disagreements became hurtful, regular fights. Eventually, my father left the family home and began a relationship with his new flame.

My mother's heart broke into a million irreparable pieces. The consolation of her husband's continued love for her did little to quiet the inner squall created by the loss of that husband's faithfulness. Her physical health mirrored her inner pain, and it appeared to my siblings and me that she was at death's door. She had spent twenty-two years as his wife, twenty-nine years in love with him, and now her identity was uncertain. Who was she, if not Mrs. Clive Daly?

It was difficult for my brothers Desmond and Walter to maintain a steady relationship with both of my parents separately. The easiest thing to do would have been to side with my mother. She was the one who was cheated on and left after a lifetime of marriage. Yet, we all loved my father and could see his side of everything. Trying to stay with a partner who expresses her anger and hurt with a drink in her hand is not an easy feat, even if you're not being tempted toward an affair.

The cloud of guilt, worry, and regret that seemed to hang over us all during this time darkened. I was happy to be traveling as much as I was but wished I could be with my family more, both the family there in England and the one I'd left behind. I thought of Cathy and Gary often, not wanting my marriage to slip away any farther than it already had. There were many nights when tears streamed down my cheeks as I lay in bed alone, and some nights when I was not alone but felt so anyway. It was more important than ever to get back to Cathy, but I couldn't make it happen and was worried she had stopped trying altogether.

Around the time my father packed his bags, I received a petition for divorce in the mail. The hope of my wife and child joining me, or my returning to them, dissolved in an instant. I felt somewhat blindsided but, in that moment, not entirely shocked.

The phone calls with Cathy had become shorter and colder. We discussed Gary, money, and little else. While I was unsurprised, I was devastated. With a few diversions to drink and take fun risks, I had been working toward the ultimate goal of reuniting with my little family somehow. That goal was now gone. I went from a man on a mission to one with nothing to fight for. There was nothing in my way, at the point, to stop me from fully surrendering to the addictions I had begun to develop.

I would still send weekly child support. Gary was still mine, after all. My role as Cathy's husband may have been coming to an end, but that could never stop me from being a father to my son. Even across the sea in another country, I could hold onto that. Somewhere, whether it was in my heart or mind I'm not sure, I held out a small grain of hope that by continuing to show Cathy that I was capable of taking care of our little one, she could find love for me again. I knew it was unrealistic to want that from her, but a man cannot survive without something to long for.

All at once, so many of my family members were falling apart. My frequent delivery trips around the country were a break from the process of group mourning. I wanted to douse my own pain in liquor and denial; confronting my parents and their problems would have made that more difficult. So, I kept myself moving. Driving, delivery, drinking; I repeated this process over and over again, waiting to feel whole. Once I was whole, I could be stronger for everyone else. I had no idea how long it would take me to get to that point.

CHAPTER EIGHT

The righteous cry, and the LORD heareth, and delivereth them out of
all their troubles.
The LORD is nigh unto them that are of a broken heart;
and saveth such as be of a contrite spirit.
Many are the afflictions of the righteous: but the LORD delivereth him out
of them all.
He keepeth all his bones: not one of them is broken.
PSALMS 34:17–20

THE FIRST TIME I went to Northern Ireland to visit my son, I was concerned how things between Cathy and I would go. I ached to see Gary's face and missed the comfort of Cathy's love. Even though I could be with Gary, it seemed I would never regain what I once had with my wife. My ex-wife. While I packed my bags, I cried. I cried for Cathy, for the son I barely knew. Tears fell for the life I had but couldn't hold on to. Most of the time, I was able to distract myself away from these thoughts, but when this first visit drew closer, they grew more difficult to silence.

Cathy had made a promise to me that I would never be kept from my son. I was grateful for that promise and appreciated her ability to respect my role as father. It gave me an inkling of hope that somewhere in her heart still lingered a bit of love for me. Concern still loomed, promise or no promise. There was bound to be some amount of tension seeing her again. If her parents or other family members were around when I arrived, there would be more tension than I could deal with alone. My heart was broken, and I did not feel strong enough to face my former in-laws. Not without a drink in me, at least, and I planned on being stone sober while spending precious time with Gary.

I had the reunion with Cathy so built up in my mind. A series of worst-case scenarios played on a loop during the short flight from England to Belfast. The knots were taut within my stomach as I arrived at Cathy's home. I was ready to see my son but could never be ready for a stressful confrontation if one happened. Cathy answered the door, and we exchanged cold pleasantries. There was no yelling, no crying, and no accusations. My former wife handed me my little son, who was unsure who I was, and told me when to bring him back to her. It was quick and anticlimactic. There's little emotional satisfaction in stoic denial, but it makes everyone's life easier in the moment.

I turned my attentions and energy to Gary. His familiarity with me, or the memory of Cathy telling him who he would be spending the day with, kicked in; he started calling me Dad. The first time that small word came out of his mouth that day, everything lightened. The worries about Cathy, the broken heart, and the uncertainty ceased to matter. My son and I were watching a football match together for the first time. We talked about the game and other harmless things. His love was so pure and innocent that it refreshed my spirit. Time with him untied those continual inner knots better than any lager or strange woman ever had.

The knots retightened, this time reaching into my heart, when it came time to hand him back to Cathy. Once again, little emotion passed between us. There were so many things I wanted to say to her. Apologies and explanations didn't seem like enough to fix what was broken, so I kept all these words to myself and gave Gary back. She had kept her promise of allowing me to see him, and that was a step in the right direction. I couldn't ask any more from her. The door to the house closed, and I left, shattered all over again by the realization that the potential of my young family had slipped away. I was more alone than ever.

Then, I met Davina. She was a neighbor of Walter's. I met her while visiting him in Tyning near Radstock. Introductions were exchanged, and I was soon informed she had taken a liking to me. I was equally attracted to her. Similar to Cathy and the stranger at the bar, Davina was another tall, slim blonde. She had a strong but warm disposition. I was immediately drawn to her.

Our relationship developed quickly. There was an unabashed honesty to the way she dealt with me. Right away, she made it very clear that she did not approve of my penchant for drinking and carrying on. She might have succeeded in pushing me into better habits had my job not taken me away from her so much. The frequent trips kept any advice and guidance she offered me from sinking in. I did feel the love she gave me, though. The excitement I felt at finding this good woman who cared for me made me impulsive.

Davina and I moved in together not long after we started seriously dating. Our home was very small, just two humble rooms. It felt like a palace to me when I was actually there. It was more privacy than I'd had in years. No more staying with family or boarding with strangers; I was making a life together with a fantastic woman who loved me. Another fresh start, another dream to chase.

My job was a challenge for us right from the start. I was gone for days at a time working, and when I got home, all I wanted to do was relax with a drink. Or several drinks. While I was not being unfaithful to Davina with another woman, a part of me was having an affair with alcohol. When faced with a choice between making her happy and having a drink at the pub with my friends, oftentimes I would choose the drink. I was putting Davina second, which wasn't fair to her.

Two months into living together, the unfairness got the best of Davina. While I was away working, Davina cheated on me. Before I could hear the story from anyone else, my honest girlfriend sat me down and confessed her mistake. She felt abandoned and frustrated; the companionship had made her feel better. Without hesitation, I forgave her. The blunt emotional bareness of her open admissions struck me. I could not look at her there, candid and contrite, and deny her my forgiveness. The man she had carried on with was another story. I found him soon after Davina's confession. He was sitting on his motorbike, readying himself to pass through an intersection. I charged at him, dragged him off the motorbike, and kicked him to the ground. He took the beating and knew its reason. I let the anger I had at myself for neglecting Davina and at Davina for giving in to her loneliness pour out of my body in this violent outburst.

I was presented with a similar temptation when I met a woman at The Railway public house, the pub near my apartment. She was my usual type: thin, blonde, and vivacious. We drank together and found we had a shared love of music and dancing. I made arrangements to meet her back at The Railway so I could show her my favorite reggae club in Bristol. It would be a night of those two shared passions, but the implication of our lusty ulterior motives was clear. When I arrived back at the small apartment I shared with Davina that night, the guilt of the date I had planned with the new woman forced me to come clean to my girlfriend. She was no angrier than she had been at the long hours spent at the bar, and we figured out how to make the situation right. I didn't want to stand this nice girl up at the reggae club. Instead, I brought Davina with me. At no point in our initial meeting had this woman asked me if I was spoken for, nor had I asked her. I could alter the tone of the night spent dancing to one of friendship, not romance. However, when my new "friend" saw me approaching with Davina on my arm, she jumped into her car and drove away. I felt bad for the girl, but not bad enough to ruin the evening. I got drunk and danced with the woman I loved, who refrained from scolding me for the night.

Davina and I settled into a routine. I worked hard, drank harder. She tried her best to find happiness with what she could not control, which was me. The love was real and very strong. If she had loved me any less, she would have run away long before we were living together. She could see through my bravado to the knots and disappointment, depression, and fear inside. I wanted to be better for her, but I wanted to drink more.

A man I worked with named Larry was going through a difficult divorce similar to what my parents and then I had dealt with. I had introduced him to my mother so that they could keep one another company while their hearts healed. They hit it off, and I began spending even more time with Larry as a result. He, like both my mother and I, was a heavy drinker. Larry and I would finish a day's work, quickly change clothes, and meet back at the pub until it closed. I was glad to know the man who was taking care of my mother, getting her back to the living world with the rest of us. It also meant I was spending time with family while I hid out at the pub, and that couldn't be a bad thing. That's what my logic told me, anyway.

Continually, Davina challenged my choices. My continued drinking gave rise to a tense home environment, which drove me to stay away as often as I could. The cycle was infuriating. I felt it turning around us and could do nothing to stop it. Davina gave me so many chances to admit my weakness and ask her for help; she would beg me to stay home after work with her. When the pleas started, I would get angry. My voice would get louder as her requests became more insistent. I met her ultimatums with pigheadedness, never willing to stray from my plans. She always backed down, too emotionally exhausted to fight back. Then I would leave her there, alone with nothing to do but cultivate resentments and more frustration.

After five years of deep love and deeper disappointments, the inevitable consequence of my cyclical behavior came to fruition. The route I drove as a council refuse truck driver took me right past where Davina and I lived. One day as I drove up to our residence, I noticed our furniture outside by the gutter. I got out of the lorry and started arguing with Davina's sister-in-law, who was helping my girlfriend move all of her belongings to the street. Davina was leaving me. Half a decade of my addictions and neglect had finally outweighed the love she had for me, and it was over. I squalled at them both, asserting they could not do this to me. How could she break my heart like this?

Davina and her sister-in-law made it clear to me that I had done this to myself, and no amount of screaming could convince her to stay with me. I got back into my truck and drove away, unable to watch Davina's worldly possessions slowly stack up on the side of the road. I thought about everything else I had lost since I had come to England. My wife had divorced me, my son barely recognized me as his father, my parents' marriage had disintegrated, and my family was growing tired of me. I cried heavy tears and thought how much easier these problems would seem if I could just disappear. My death would remove me from the knots that tightened and made me drink, made me angry and afraid. These thoughts accelerated when I saw a large lorry driving towards me on the opposite side of the road. The council-owned refuse van I was in would be smashed into by the larger delivery truck, surely killing me inside of it. I could turn the wheel right now, drive into the path of the lorry. It all seemed very neat and easy. No more pain, no more rejection. You can't leave a dead man.

My hands tightened on the steering wheel. My vision tunneled, and all I saw was the approaching lorry. I did not think of the driver's life or the damage a crash like this would cause. I waited for the exact right moment to move my vehicle into the truck's path, and in those seconds, the image of my mother's face and the sound of her sad, quiet voice overtook all other thoughts. The death of one of her children would be devastating; losing a son in this way would destroy her once and for all. Her heart couldn't take another tragedy. My innocent son Gary, who had done nothing to deserve pain, would be left without a father. If I committed suicide, it would create a domino effect. No family can be the same after an event like this, especially not one as fragile as mine.

I loosened my grip on the wheel and continued driving on the correct side of the road. Of course, I wound up at the pub. A huge part of me was missing again. The hole Davina had filled in my spirit was vacant. Now I had no one to go home to, no one waiting for me to leave the bar.

CHAPTER NINE

Be sober, be vigilant; because your adversary the devil, as a roaring lion,
walketh about, seeking whom he may devour:
1 PETER 5:8

I SAT IN MY BOSS'S office with hands wringing in my lap, trying my best to maintain eye contact despite the anger and surprise fighting to find a voice inside me. The attendance record for the several years I'd spent hauling refuse in a council lorry was sitting on the desk between us. I had missed thirty-six Monday shifts over the past year, plus a few other random days. After four and a half years of service, I was being let go due to my unreliability. There was nothing I could offer in my own defense; the evidence of my absenteeism was right there in the official record.

It was the drinking that kept me from showing up for work Mondays. Hangovers always feel worse an hour before you're scheduled to work, especially if that work involves a hot refuse van, manual labor, and long hours. Davina had been gone for a few weeks, my contact with Gary was neglected and irregular, and now I was unemployed again at the age of twenty-nine.

A family friend and fellow binge drinker, Andrew, had a rental property in Westfield, near Radstock. He allowed me to live there, as long as I could keep up with the monthly bills. I moved in and fell into the same pattern of sleeping all day and drinking all night that I had when I first arrived in England seven years earlier.

Andrew was a good friend and a better drinking partner. Like so many of the important people in my life at the time, Andrew and I bonded over a shared love of music and movies. Night after night, the two of us would watch our favorite movies over and over after stumbling back from a pub. He never questioned or judged the hours I spent on a barstool. The friendship between Andrew and I was the perfect storm of alcohol and fearlessness. The unemployment benefits I quickly started receiving was meant to pay for my food and housing but was more often handed over to the variety of public houses Andrew and I haunted. When the ends didn't quite meet and I needed more cash to keep partying at the end of the month, I would beg and borrow.

Recklessness felt good.

The mixture of alcohol, uncertainty, and danger deadened the tension of my inner knots and filled my thoughts with hedonism, leaving no room for depression or regret. In the mornings, when the painful brightness of sun irritated my hangover and alcohol withdrawal, I would be reminded that the knots were still there, waiting. A quick pull of hard cider for breakfast fixed that right up, and I would wander back into another day of aimless revelry.

I spent several hours on the worst days piecing together the events of the previous night. Friends, neighbors, and even some strangers provided me with foggy puzzle pieces of what I had done or said. My own memory had, at this point, become entirely unreliable. Nights bled into one another, a single never-ending loop. If it weren't for onlookers describing exactly how I had danced on the tables, whom I had picked a fight with, and where I had been barred from, I never would have known.

One typical Sunday afternoon, Andrew and I were heading to the Burberry Club, a snooker club at which he and I had developed a reputation for rowdiness. At that time, pubs in England still kept strict, specific hours of operation. The doors would open to the public at eleven in the morning, close at three in the afternoon, and then reopen for the evening shift that ran from seven to eleven at night. Every day at 3:00 p.m., last orders were called, which is right when Andrew and I approached the front door of the Burberry Club.

The door was locked, so we knocked. The bartender on duty pointed to the clock and said they were closed. I knocked louder and cupped my hands between the glass paned door and my eyes to get a better view inside. At the bar were several men, drinking their pints and smiling. They were laughing at Andrew and me, mocking our inability to join them inside, I was sure of it. Then, as if the imagined taunting wasn't enough to push me to rage, the bartender pulled a draft of lager for one of those grinning patrons. If they were closed and last orders had been called, why was he serving another pint?

As that glass of after-call beer hit the bar, I decided if my friend and I were unable to drink, no one would be able to drink. My fun Sunday afternoon of drinking was ruined, and so everyone else at Burberry Club would have his day ruined as well. I wound back and punched my callused fist straight through the pane of glass separating me from my alcohol, from my numbness. The placement of the punch was poorly thought out, and I hit the lower half of the glass, which immediately shattered and fell onto my exposed hand, wrist, and arm. Screams of surprise, not fear, rang through the pub. Everyone in there knew us, Andrew and I, and was aware we were more harm to ourselves than anyone else.

Blood ran down my arm in thin tendrils. I hadn't expected such a deep gash or so much blood. Someone who knew me must have called my mother to alert the family of my injury. The next thing I remember is Walter pulling up in his car to rescue me. He drove me to the closest hospital a bloody, still angry, mess.

The shattered glass had cut a vein in my arm. It took several stitches to close it up properly. So much blood was lost that I needed to stay in that hospital for four days. Once again, I found myself listening to a doctor tell me how lucky I was to be alive, that I should be more careful and cut back on the alcohol. As usual, I nodded in understanding and thanked God for my life but with no real plans on changing a thing. An alarm clock was going off, trying to wake me from my waking sleep of numbness, and I hit the snooze button.

It was raining, and I was drunk. Somewhere among the public houses I was bouncing between, I had gotten turned around. I wasn't entirely sure which direction would take me back home. The rain was freezing cold, which chilled my pickled brain, confusing me even more. I wandered down an alley in hopes of getting my bearings. This was no help, however, and I was too tired to keep trying new directions at random. A rubbish skip full of newspaper and cardboard scraps caught my eye. It looked dry, warm, and best of all, close by. Thankfully, my arm had completely healed, and I used it to give myself a boost into the skip. I laid back into the garbage, which was just as dry and warm as I had hoped.

Before long, I was fast asleep.

The next morning I awoke to a refuse worker securing the net over the skip. Had I woken up a few minutes later, I would have been dumped or crushed along with the trash I'd made into my bed.

"Oy!" I screamed at top of my lungs.

The man yelled and jumped, very startled by the unexpected human voice. As a former refuse worker myself, I can understand his immediate fear. One never expects to find a man in a rubbish skip, especially not a living man. He helped me out and on my way, while I apologized weakly. It was only after several sober years were behind me that I realized how easily a sleeping man can be devoured by a landfill, never to be seen again, and how lucky I was to walk away that morning.

CHAPTER TEN

*Beloved, think it not strange concerning the fiery trial which is to try you,
as though some strange thing happened unto you: But rejoice, inasmuch as ye
are partakers of Christ's sufferings; that, when his glory shall be revealed, ye
may be glad also with exceeding joy.*
1 PETER 4:12–13

T HE LEASE ON THE Westfield house was up, and it was time
to move on.

I found myself homeless and running out of viable options.
Andrew, who hadn't wanted to leave a good friend without a
place to rest his head, offered me a converted garage apartment
for smaller monthly fee. This new home consisted of two small
bedrooms, a bathroom, and a combination living space and
kitchen. Despite the extra space available, I relegated my life to
the single bedroom and kitchen area. Each day was essentially
identical; I would roll my cigarettes from cheap tobacco, cook
my steady diet of boiled potatoes and plain buttered bread, and
escape the silent house for more distracting activities. Life as
Andrew's tenant and friend meant I could continue to live as
though losing Cathy, Gary, Davina, and myself never mattered.

The King's Arm was a side benefit of moving into the
garage.

The popular pub was less than seventy feet from my new
home. I could spend hours there and still find my way back
without getting lost or accidentally crushed to death in a rubbish

skip. I knew the staff, the other regulars, and how far I could push them before being asked to leave.

On a night in 1997, much like the dozens of nights before it, my brother James, cousin Robert, and friend Mike had joined me at the King's Arm to prowl for women. My young body was absorbing the abuse of minimal food and maximum alcohol with little visible damage. The women who spotted me moving to music and laughing with friends in the smoky pub lighting saw a confident, if somewhat out of control, force of nature. I groomed my long black hair in a sleek ponytail, wore fashionably tight clothing, and went out of my way to draw and keep the attention of every female I could find. Flirting and dancing with girls gave energy to my nights of drinking and company to celebrate.

After spending a short time fruitlessly looking for the night's ingénues, my companions and I decided a change of scenery was called for. I'm not sure who suggested the Fir Tree Pub, but we piled into Mike's car. I got in the back passenger seat beside James, Mike was driving, and Robert rode as the front passenger. The Fir Tree was a short drive through a double roundabout and, even though Mike had a drink or two at King's Arm, none of us was drunk.

We navigated the first roundabout easily, Mike shifting his car from third to second gear to accelerate through the next turn. The four of us saw the car coming over the next hill toward the roundabout but did not notice the drunk driver swerving and losing control. Mike's car was struck on the passenger side, right on the center frame that divided the front and back seats. The world around me spun and then darkened for a moment as the car was thrown from the road and flipped upside down. Mike and Robert were pinned in the crushed front half of the car but were kept alive by the seatbelts they had thought to fasten before we got moving. James hadn't worn his for what should have been a short and easy ride. Disoriented and concerned about police arriving at the accident, I told my brother to run away to avoid getting in trouble. I held my left hand to a wound on my fore-head that was pouring blinding blood into my eyes as I fumbled with my cell phone to call an ambulance. Mike looked okay, but Robert wasn't moving. Memories of childhood adventures, Robert by my side, flooded my crisis-heightened thoughts. The ambulance came and removed my two cousins from the demolished vehicle. The three of us were taken to the hospital. As the passengers on the side that was hit, Robert and I had received the worst of the injuries. My split open head was inspected, cleaned, and sealed with liquid stitches. An unmistakable scar still marks my forehead. Robert was much worse off with a possible broken neck. The two of us were held for observation, to make sure the injuries were under control. None of us was charged with a crime; it was obvious to the police that the other driver was seriously intoxicated and had been the one at fault.

Robert recovered well, and soon we were causing trouble from our respective hospital beds. Both of us had voracious cigarette appetites and, as any smoker will understand, the constant nicotine cravings transformed us into mewling, inconsolable children. The seriousness of the accident paled in comparison to the tragedy of being trapped in a hospital bed for days without a smoke. My cousin and I made juvenile sport of harassing the nurses for the chance to smoke the cigarettes we wanted. The frustrated nurses were no match for the squalling Robert and I were capable of, and we got our way. In a hospital today, this would never happen, but the nurses wheeled the two of us outside, beds and all. Pride at our victory and the thrill of surviving the crash inspired waves of shared laughter as Robert, my beloved childhood mate and cousin, and I puffed away at forbidden cigarettes.

Shortly after moving into that garage, I heard my cousin Eddy was moving back to Northern Ireland. His brother Brian cleared his flat out and had a pile of things ready to be thrown away. Amongst the discarded belongings was a battered King James Bible.

"Can I have that?" I asked, pointing to the Bible.

Brian let me take it. It would have just been thrown out with the rest if I hadn't. My memories of religion and God that had stayed with me since childhood kept me from letting a Holy Bible wind up in a pile of rotted vegetables and moldy newspapers in the nearest garbage tip.

Most of the language was inscrutable to me, so many *thous* and *thees*. The stories and the scenery called to me, though. Many nights, as I sat drunk and bored, alone in my dimly lit room, I would thumb through the pages, finding sections I could understand. The rows of olive trees, peaceful expanses of sandy deserts, and the rolling waters of the Sea of Galilee were pictured so clearly in my mind as I worked my way through that Bible. I imagined standing on the Mount of Beatitudes, taking in the same views of Israel Jesus Christ had seen as He preached his lessons to the mass of believers. That world of peace, faith, and beauty felt a million miles away from where I was in that converted bungalow garage. Israel was not the place for me. My place was on a barstool at the local pub, not in the Holy Land.

Sometime in the early morning hours on January 24, 2000, I was driving home from my barstool to read more from that Bible and then go to sleep. The drive had taken me through the village of Shepton Mallet. This low-income, rough, residential village was about twelve miles from my home. I was drunk that night, and the memory of where I was driving from and which friend was in the passenger seat next to me have long faded into the fog my memories of that time often form. I do clearly remember the flashing blue lights of the police car that pulled up behind me, though.

The restrictions I was forced to comply with after my first DR10 were a fresh memory, and I had no intention of undergoing a test of my sobriety. I was more than drunk; I was wasted. There was no good, justifiable reason for me to have been behind the wheel of my car. Of course, the officer would recognize my intoxication, and a second drunk-driving offense would be guaranteed. Instead of pulling over to the side of the road, I turned into a rank of council houses, hoping to evade the larger, slower police car. The street I had taken ended up turning back on itself in a dead end. My getaway route ended in a quaint cul-de-sac. I was trapped. The police car blocked my ability to turn around and try a new path; my only remaining option to get away was to flee on foot. My run was quickly ended when my sloppy, drunken strides caused me to trip over my own feet. I fell face first onto the front lawn of some suburban stranger.

The officers who had been chasing me brought me to my feet and began asking me a series of questions. Suddenly, my detainment in New Castle when I was seventeen and the violence I experienced at the hands of the police took over the portion of my rational judgment not being controlled by alcohol. I refused to answer their questions, balked at the breathalyzer test when it was requested, and put up as much of a fight as I could before they loaded me into the back of their car.

I hoped as we drove to the closest police station, which was in Yeovil and a long car ride away, that the time passing would help to sober me up. Perhaps the charges against me would include evading the police or some driving offense, but not another troublesome DR10. Once at the station, I was escorted to get my blood drawn and tested. The legal blood alcohol level limit is 80 mg; my blood test came back showing a blood alcohol level of 160 mg. I was over the legal limit by double, and there was no escaping the drunk-driving charge leveled against me.

As the second DR10 I was convicted of, the penalties were harsher. I was sentenced to a three-year license disqualification, minus nine months if I completed an alcohol and drunken driving awareness course. I also had to pay a £60 fine and the court costs. The judge warned that if I found myself back in front of him on another DR10 charge, he would make sure I spent plenty of time in prison sobering up.

Not long after my sentencing, I found myself at the University of Bath in a classroom with about twenty other men. We had all been convicted of nearly identical charges, mostly driving while intoxicated. The class focused on movies depicting the consequences of drinking and getting behind the wheel. In a dark room, surrounded by strangers, I blankly watched the screen flash images of fiery car crashes and maimed bodies with their faces blurred for privacy. The movie was meant to wake us up, make us cognizant of the impact our actions could have on ourselves, our loved ones, and perfectly innocent strangers. I wish I could say I had been affected, moved, or anything more than bored and impatient. Classrooms, so much like that one at the University of Bath, had always been simultaneously peaceful and stimulating safe havens for me. That was no longer the case. The endless hours of sitting still and quiet were triggering the part of me that needed movement and a pint of lager. I walked out of the alcohol awareness class with little more than the satisfaction of having nine months knocked off my driving restriction.

My mother and stepfather Larry took over The Railway public house on Wells Road, right down the road from where Davina and I had shared a home for five years, and a few street numbers away from Andrew's small converted bungalow. The yellowish building hugged the corner of Wells Road in Radstock where I had considered ending my life in a car crash, and The Railway itself had been the scene of many drunken nights.

It seemed surreal to see my diminutive mother behind that bar serving drinks and keeping order, and even more preposterous was my eventual migration to one of the small rooms above the business. My unemployment benefits had been stretched too thin, and the rent I had to pay Andrew became impossible. A thirty-something-year-old man should be building a life with a wife and children. Instead of that idyllic scenario, I was crawling back to my mother as an aimless and homeless drunk. The regression to needy child did not trouble me. Instead, I found an easy comfort in my room above the bar. Below me was all the booze I could ever want, and down the hall was a loving mother who would never kick me out. It was safe and certain, which is all I wanted then.

Andrew and my other mates were also quick supporters of my new accommodation. Sneaking down to the closed down Railway after my mother had locked up and gone to bed was a regular activity for Andrew and me. The movie *Highlander* is much more fun the hundredth time you've seen it if you've nicked a free bottle of Bacardi from your mother's business.

On a regular night of drinking, listening to music, and watching movies with Andrew, the burglar alarm malfunctioned and began to sound. We hadn't set it off; neither Andrew nor I were careless enough to trigger the obvious alarm. I went to the back hallway that led to the residence space Larry, my mother, and I shared. That is where the alarm box had been installed.

My mother had beaten me to the alarm.

The sound had jarred her from sleep. In one small, delicate hand, she clutched a baseball bat nearly as big as she was, for protection and defense. The other pounded at the keys of the alarm box, trying to disable the noise. Larry mustn't have given her the new disarm code, and her button pushing was accomplishing nothing. An exacerbated but feminine grunt escaped her frowning lips. The frustration became too much, and she began beating the bat against the small metal box.

While it was happening, and later up in my room recounting it with Andrew, this scene was the most uproariously hilarious moment I had ever witnessed. Most patrons of the bar, most people she had ever met, in fact, would never conceive my mother capable of such unexpected violent outbursts. It was comical and adorable at the same time.

Retrospect can be a sobering thing, though.

The alarm had not been the only frustrating influence that night. That woman's eldest son was so far gone in drink that he saw nothing wrong with meandering into his mother's place of work and outright stealing her livelihood from under her. Her son, who was precious Gary's father, was a drunk, dependent on her kindness and spare room. Every strike of that bat against the denting alarm box was a strike against her powerlessness to save me, my helplessness to save myself, and the sickness that she kept safely guarded, the same sickness that was running my every waking moment.

My mother had no patience for her boisterous sons creating a ruckus in her bar. She tried to make it very clear to us that The Railway was not our personal playground; the same rules that applied at bars not owned by our mother applied there as well. The same stern looks and iron rule she used to reign in unruly customers were used to keep James and me in line as well.

After helping Larry put away and display a new shipment of Diamond White cider, I decided to enjoy a few of the bottles. I hadn't meant to get as drunk as I did; the sweetened cider drink had higher alcohol content than others I'd had before. As my voice grew louder and more slurred, my mother became more irritated. In front of the crowd of patrons, some of them my friends, she cut me off and told me to leave.

My body was enflamed by embarrassment at being scolded like a child in front of friends, strangers, and a few women I wouldn't have minded sharing a dance with. Take the Diamond White away from me, I thought, then no one could enjoy it. I stormed off behind the bar, extended my arm, and swept the remaining fifty bottles to the floor. My mother's stunned face was momentarily motionless as she stared at the pile of broken glass and pooling cider that could have been money in her pocket. The surprise wore off quickly, and she exploded in anger that roared louder than mine. She screamed at me as I left the bar for my room upstairs, insisting I would pay her back. Already, I felt foolish and mean, and her hurt yelling drove those terrible feelings deeper.

My brother James was also prone to getting barred by our mother. During one of his worst nights of rowdy partying, she had had enough of him and asked me to get him out of her sight.

"Do something with him," she muttered, pointing to James.

I stepped in as the big brother, prodding him into intoxicated anger. I was far from sober myself, and the attempt to get James to leave eroded into an all-out fight. I drew back to punch James and missed. My hand struck the wooden frame of the window behind him. Aside from a small cut on the knuckle of my pinky finger, my hand felt fine. The missed hit broke up the brotherly scrap. I left James at the bar and went to bed. The next morning, I woke up and checked out how the small knuckle wound was healing. Instead of the reddish brown scab I expected to see forming, there was a black spot. Everyone knows black is a bad sign, so I quickly got dressed and went to the doctor.

The local doctor took one look at the small black spot and called an ambulance to take me to the hospital. There was an infection, a bad one, that had swiftly taken hold and was spreading. Had I tried to wait it out, it would have inked through my bloodstream and to my heart. Once that kind of infection hits an alcohol-weakened bloodstream, death is guaranteed. I was admitted to the hospital for immediate and hardline treatment.

An extraordinarily strong antibiotic called erythromycin was administered into my blood through a constant IV flow. The doctors and nurses said it was helping to cure me, but it felt as though hot, jagged sand was being pushed through my veins. Detox was just as excruciating as the medicine, and all I wanted was to tear that little plastic tube out of my arm and find the closest pub willing to serve a man in a hospital gown. When withdrawal from nicotine and alcohol wasn't keeping me in a restless sleep, I screamed in pain for hours on end. Death seemed like a beautiful respite, and I begged for the antibiotics to fail, allowing the infection to stop my heart.

Then, it was over. After sixteen days and several surgeries, the infection abated, the IV came out, and my finger was showing signs of healing. Before being released back into my life, the doctor came to take off the splint that had been put on my little finger to help it heal. Without the bracing holding it in a normally straight position, my pinky stuck out at an odd angle. When I tried to close my hand into a fist, that deformed little finger refused to bend. It would be permanent, the doctor surmised. If I ever tried to punch someone in the face again, I'd wind up poking him in the eye instead.

CHAPTER ELEVEN

Wherefore he saith, Awake thou that sleepest, and arise from the dead,
and Christ shall give thee light.
See then that ye walk circumspectly, not as fools, but as wise,
Redeeming the time, because the days are evil.
Wherefore be ye not unwise, but understanding what the
will of the Lord is.
And be not drunk with wine, wherein is excess; but be
filled with the Spirit.
EPHESIANS 5:14–18

M Y LONG BLACK HAIR and unique features opened the door to small film roles that helped me earn money on a more regular basis. This new income encouraged me to find a home of my own. The housing council had denied me accommodation, reminding me over and over that a single man with no family was not a housing priority. I was annoyed and frustrated by that decision; I had a son who would visit me at some point, after all. Plus, I had put my life in danger serving my country when it would have been much easier and safer to avoid aligning myself with the armed forces. I deserved a place to call home, especially since I could finally afford it.

I took it upon myself to go over the local council's head and wrote a strongly worded letter to Parliament's House of Commons in London. My arguments must have been persuasive, as I soon was granted accommodation in a small, one-bedroom apartment in Peasedown, St. John in late July 2001. It had everything I needed. The perfect quiet place that was mine and mine alone.

––––––––––––––

Robert and I went on holiday to Northern Ireland soon after my second arrest and conviction, only a few days after I had finished moving into my new apartment. I had spent so much time making obligatory trips back and forth for an endless string of family funerals, that the chance to spend time there outside of a graveyard was impossible to pass up. I would have Robert with me, so the inconvenience of the driving ban could do little to interfere with our vacation. I would be able to spend time with Gary, now nearly a grown man at seventeen years old, and Robert would see his twin daughters.

I made plans to stay with my cousin Ronnie, Robert had other lodging plans, and off we went to visit our children. All three of them were old enough to accompany us to pubs and nightclubs, so I was able to combine my two great passions. My first love was Gary, no matter how much time or distance separated us. Next was the beautifully knot-loosening force of alcohol and the boisterous social attention it brought into my orbit. I was buzzing to share that special experience with my son, to show him what I believed was the best version of me.

The nightclubbing was a success. My son and I laughed together, sincere rolling laughter, for the first time in years. Though I knew a night of partying wasn't the traditional father-son bonding exercise, it felt good and right. I saw so many small movements Gary made, in his storytelling and the way he spoke to girls, that was almost like looking in a mirror at my teenage self. It was worth leaving my comfort zone of England for the uneasiness Northern Ireland always made me feel. The streets may have been calmer, renegade bombs and bullets were less common by then, but the memories of my youth were still there, making me on edge. Enough alcohol and time spent watching my son have fun alongside me quelled that edginess to a faraway throb.

Once Robert, the twins, Gary, and I were done living it up,

I drove us back to Ronnie's house. I had borrowed Ronnie's car and had to move it back to its rightful spot in the driveway between two stone pillars. Lingering self-confidence left over from drinking, dancing, and fun with my son convinced me that I could easily navigate the tricky turn straight on. Gary's eyes lit up when he bragged that his dad was a professional driver. The sound of him calling me his dad coupled with the gushing pride of his boasts pushed me to get behind the wheel, driving ban forgotten in exchange for my need to show off. Gary took the front passenger seat to witness his professional driver father back a car between two solid structures with no trouble. I began backing up and everything seemed under control and easy to handle. As I maneuvered the front end of the car between the stone objects, I thought I had it lined up well enough to make it through.

I was wrong. The passenger side of the car made hard, scraping impact with the wall. Gary jumped and let out a small, muffled yell. We both cursed, and my face flushed in embarrassment. Gary's eyes were large, dilated, and childlike. His unbelieving face reminded me of the picture his mother had sent me over a decade before, a Christmas picture of Gary standing with Cathy and her new husband. That picture made me feel insignificant, and watching all the pride Gary had in my driving ability melt away brought that feeling right back. I was out of control and had no business caring for Gary, even if he was already grown up.

Less than a month after returning from this disastrous visit with my son, Cathy called me. She wanted to change Gary's last name to that of her second husband. They had two younger sons with that name, she had changed hers, and of course there was Gary's adoptive father at the head of the pack. Gary alone had a differing surname and, according to Cathy, this had prompted other children to tease Gary with bullying, hurtful questions, and taunts. I was sensitive to his situation but did not want to let go of the last real connection I had with my son, my precious namesake. Since Gary was still a minor, Cathy needed my permission to have his name changed. My first impulse was to outright deny her request and berate her for even asking for such a hurtful and demeaning favor. Yet, I knew if I followed that gut reaction, I could jeopardize the tenuous relationship I still had with Gary and the access to my son Cathy still granted. The compromise I was able to submit to was asking to discuss this with Gary before a final decision was made. If I heard from my son the same reasoning and explanation for the change of name, I would give my permission.

When I spoke to Gary, he echoed his mother almost exactly. My slightly paranoid reasoning told me that a seventeen–year-old young man was not bothered by childish taunts and an underlying motivation to change his name from Daly was not being shared. In an effort to endear myself to my nearly adult child, I gave in. My namesake vanished with a single signed document, and my heart broke once again. Alcohol did little to numb this pain, which was manageable with time but never truly healed.

———————————

Everything began to change on June 5, 2002.

A friend, not a close one but one I enjoyed spending time with at the pub, invited me to the town of Weston-super-Mare. The small town by the ocean was a popular vacation destination and was a great place to spend a weekend in bars flirting with traveling women. Another tragic family death less than six months prior had left me feeling somewhat empty, and the chance to disappear to Weston-super-Mare sounded like a way to replace that emptiness with more hedonistic feelings.

The only problem was I still had no employment, plus my court cost debts and unyielding lifestyle rendered me cash-poor. I could never afford the cost of an expensive beachside hotel room, the cost of parking my car for two to three days, or the price of public transport. My friend solved that problem by offering me a free parking spot and lodging at the apartment he shared with another man. It would be no problem, my easygoing mate assured me; his roommate wouldn't mind one bit. I celebrated my good fortune by packing a small bag with the essentials and driving straight to the beach. When I arrived at the three-story apartment building where I was meant to be staying, my friend greeted me warmly. I took a quick shower, he and I shared several quick drinks, and we left for our favorite pastime—pub crawling.

Early summer was one of Weston-super-Mare's busiest times; the newly warm weather drew out hundreds of tourists seeking a good time and sunshine. The bars were packed that night. I lost track of my inebriated host in the undulating crowds that moved to and from the bar top like the waves that were crashing a few blocks away. I wasn't concerned; the route back to the apartment was easy enough to remember, and I was sure we would meet back up by the end of the night. The time came to call it a night, and my friend was still nowhere to be found. Again, I was not worried and assumed he had gotten tired or found a girl and would be at the apartment when I got back.

Still in high spirits and buzzing from the enveloping effects of big crowds and mixed drinks, I happily strolled back to my temporary accommodation. There was a light on in the third floor apartment when I tried to enter the building. The door was locked, so I buzzed and knocked. When there was no answer to my polite, subdued attempts to get in, I knocked harder and shouted up for my mate to open the door. No one came down, neither my companion nor the roommate he had mentioned to me. Impatience became outrage. I knocked harder and yelled louder, demanding to be let in to the apartment where my bag of clothes and toiletries were stowed. My incessant commands eventually got the attention of the person behind the window that still shone its bright incandescent light. A stranger to me, most likely the roommate of my friend, opened the window and told me the man who had invited me to stay was not there, and I had to leave. Then, my bag of clothes was tumbling down from the open window onto the street three stories down. I had to dodge it quickly to avoid taking a blow to the head and getting knocked out by my own shoes, clothes, and toothbrush.

I couldn't sleep in my car on the street; that's how a drunken man gets robbed, killed, or worse—arrested for loitering. My record would make me a prime target for any patrolling police officer who happened to find me sleeping and ran my name or license number. The small amount of pocket money I had scrounged up to bring with me had been spent at the pubs I had gone to; there wasn't even enough to pay for a pauper's bed. Despite being tipsy, the only rational option I could come up with was to chance driving home. I felt setup and betrayed by my friend, who had a lot of explaining to do if I ever saw him again. His roommate could do his explaining to the bottom of my boot, as far as I was concerned. All I wanted to do was get home and forget the entire night.

Not five minutes after moving my car out of its parking spot, a police car pulled up behind me and turned on its lights. I cursed, pounded my hand against the steering wheel, and moved my car to the side. The feeling of being set up overtook me as I was removed from my car and underwent a sobriety test. I knew I had been drinking, and the explanation I tried to offer for why I had no choice but to drive did not keep the officer from arresting me. On the drive to the jail, I catalogued all the things I would be leaving behind when the judge inevitably shipped me off to prison. A third DR10 offense certainly meant I would be serving plenty of time behind bars.

I spent the night in a jail cell. The alcohol in my bloodstream lulled me to a quick sleep, but when I woke up the next morning the world had defogged. The gravity of my situation began to take shape.

Four weeks after my arrest, I was awaiting my court date and sentencing. Something in my rational mind snapped, and I was forced to accept the reality of going to prison. I had no more fear of my impending incarceration. In prison, there would be regular meals and a roof over my head. I wouldn't need to pay rent or go to the store. The question of how I would spend my days would never bother me for the length of my sentence. It would be easier in that life. The last decade of my life had been spent searching for ease and reprieve. Perhaps a few years in prison could finally grant me that.

A week after accepting my future as a prisoner, I was cleaning in the kitchen of my small, one-bedroom flat. I had moved into this flat thanks to government benefits and an unyielding need to be on my own. The Yellow Pages phonebook was on the side of my counter and as I turned to put something away, I knocked the heavy book off the counter onto the kitchen floor. When I bent to pick the phone book up and put it back where it belonged, I noticed it had opened to the listing for Alcoholics Anonymous.

The world narrowed, focused on that small listing. For the first time, the concept of my issues being connected to alcoholism occurred as a possibility. All of the things I had lost, including the impending loss of my freedom, were connected to my love of the drink. The way I felt in the mornings or when I had gone several hours without a sip of alcohol, the habit my hands had of shaking, and my inability to remember fine details of the day before—all of these sounded like the makings of an addict. Maybe there were others out there who felt the knots tighten in their bodies and loosened them with a pint or a shot. I picked up the phone and dialed the number in the listing.

The man who answered was pleasant but serious in his tone. I told him I thought I needed help, that I thought I was an alcoholic, and that I had problem I could no longer control. After going over brief details of my situation, most importantly my lack of transport due to my recent arrest, he told me he would send out two men to pick me up and bring me to help. Images of men in hospital uniforms carting me off to a recovery center for winos and drunks sent a chill through my body, but I knew even that scenario would be better than continuing the way I had been going.

There was a call. A man from Alcoholics Anonymous had found my housing estate, Eckweek Gardens, but could not find my home. I told him to wait at the entrance and I would come to him. Unsure but hopeful, I threw on a jacket and went to meet the man who was going to attempt to help me.

I came upon a car with two men in it. When I had envisioned what the escorts from AA would look like, smiling innocent men in dress shirts and pressed pants had come to mind. This car was occupied by two rough-looking men with long hair, wearing leathers. Despite my surprise at their appearance, I got into the backseat of the car. I was scared of these men, concerned they weren't who they said they were. No proof of their connection with the treatment program had been offered, nor had I asked for any. My instincts were entirely focused on finding people who could understand the way I felt. If that meant getting in a strange car with two strange men, putting myself in potential danger, so be it. Nothing they could do to me could match what I had already done to myself.

The decision to go with the men turned out to be a safe one. No blindside beating or other dangerous trick happened; they simply took me to a small church in Bath where a nightly AA meeting was convening. At the front of the room, a boisterous man with a strong Northern Irish accent was directing everyone to sit and get ready for the meeting to start. The sound of his accent, so much like my own, eased some of my uncertainty and discomfort in the unknown surroundings. I sat near the back of the room and looked around at the people filling the chairs around me. These were not the gutter-dwelling winos I had anticipated. Some were dressed in business suits; there were women with pristine makeup framing their desperate and sad faces. Could these put-together, upper echelon people really feel the same compulsive need to drink that had brought me here? Did these businessmen and well-kept ladies have those clenching, tightening knots? As I listened to people tell their stories, I heard pieces of my own life. Broken families, lost loves, and aimless wandering from mistake to mistake were common themes in the eerily familiar monologues. Near the end of the meeting, the man leading the group asked if there was anyone else who wanted to share. I raised my hand, gave my name, and was invited to stand to address the group.

Something in me changed as I admitted to my problem for the first time. I told the strangers seated around me how I was looking at time in prison due to my drinking and other self-destructive habits. The eyes watching me speak did not make me feel judged or afraid; instead, I felt welcomed and cared for. When I left that night, I stopped in the parking lot as everyone else moved off in different directions. I raised my open palms to the sky and emphatically thanked God for bringing me to that place.

I went to meetings every night that week. The questions and discussions pushed me to understand how my life had gotten so out of control. The community flanking my fragile wellbeing gave me the strength to do the difficult work. My frequent presence in the group ingratiated me to another attendee who connected me to a community service and outpatient recovery program. Letters to the judge presiding over my case were written, shining a light on my eleventh-hour recovery plan and the effort I was finally committing to sobriety. There was hope again, hope that I could remain free and piece together a stable, sober life for myself. It was a tiny pinprick of light in a very dark situation, but the letters and my sedate resignation to a healthier life were capable of convincing the court I was no longer a danger to society.

CHAPTER TWELVE

If we confess our sins,
he is faithful and just to forgive us our sins,
and to cleanse us from all unrighteousness.
1 JOHN 1:9

W HEN I WAS YOUNG, an old man taught me the finer
points of fly fishing. On a perfect summer day years after
my last attempt at it, I tested my rusty fly fishing skills with my
cousin Brian and his son. We went to Chew Valley Lake, a combination scenic public park and private fishing lake. There was an
obviously professional fisherman posted near us, complete with
proper waders and feathered fishing cap. I was looking forward
to showing off my long-neglected casting skills and proving my
worth with my cousin and an expert in sight.

After a stream of boastful comments, I let off my first cast
and watched it fall sadly into the water no more than a foot
from where I stood. In the sharp reality of sobriety, the embarrassment of my cousin's laughter stung deeply. Brian's laughter
encouraged his son's quiet giggle to grow louder, and I saw the
experienced nearby fisherman chortle and shrug at my failure.
The person I had been a few months before would have lost his
temper and stormed from the lake in a huff of enraged humiliation. Instead, I tried my best to smile and enjoy the humor in
the moment.

I went to reel in my line and try at a second attempt. To
everyone's surprise, there was a bite on the line. My patience in

the face of mortification was rewarded with a gorgeous three-pound rainbow trout, a once in a lifetime catch. It was the first large rainbow trout I had ever caught, and the egotistical pride from before my pathetic cast was replaced with grateful pride in the unexpected blessing. I ate that trout for dinner that evening with a permanent smile on my face.

Before my previous criminal court appearances, I had taken a shot for courage and to calm my nerves. The morning of my sentencing for a third drunk-driving offense, a steadying drink was out of the question. My sobriety was new and fragile; the sentencing hearing was the first true test of my commitment.

I sat with my assigned solicitor, the three magistrates, and the judge considering the evidence of my arrest as I watched quietly. Fear that my recent efforts to get clean and change my ways would not be enough to keep me out of prison pushed and grated at my mind. By the time I was called to the stand, I felt small and helpless, like a misbehaved child. I expressed remorse for my poor choices and the dangerous decision to drive while under the influence. When asked about my recovery, I spoke of my gratitude to the program and how much I looked forward to the next three months of outpatient rehab. I was earnest and respectful; the brazen and mistrusting drunk who had been pulled over was nowhere in sight.

The magistrates left to decide my fate. The three of them, two elderly men and one elderly woman, were only away from the room for ten minutes. Each of those minutes stretched and warped into an endlessly unraveling spool of time. I stared down at my battered and scarred hands that reflected the violence of my years spent in bondage to alcohol. The possibility of going to prison was one I had come to terms with weeks before, but it was still an unwanted and unsettling prospect.

After ten minutes of anxious and interminable waiting, the magistrates filed back into the room. The decision they had reached was, shockingly, a favorable one. The letters from the treatment center and others I had been working on recovery with, combined with my remorseful admittance of my addiction, had proven to them that this was the last time I would be before the court on such a charge. The judge made it very clear to me that there were no more chances for me and sentenced me to an extended four-year driving ban and fines. I was even given the option to reduce my driving ban by an entire year by completing the same alcohol awareness course I had taken previously in Bath.

I walked out of that courthouse in Weston-super-Mare a free man.

The relief was overwhelming. Before returning to my apartment, I went to visit my mother and share the news with her. As the details of the hearing and the decision of the sentence left my mouth, every ounce of the tension that had built in me during the sentencing also left my body. My mother shared in my relief, and we quietly celebrated my freedom. I went home after a short visit. By the time I reached the front door of the apartment, I was exhausted. Fear has an ability to drain energy from each muscle and render you a helpless crawling pile of a man. How I managed to move from the front door to my bedroom is still a mystery to me. I had run from the police, climbed the side of a building, and nearly drowned in my life, yet that evening after my sentencing remains the most drained I had ever been.

I stood on unsteady legs in the center of my bedroom, crying hot tears. The sobs were animalistic, pained, and unrestrained. I had nothing left in me to hold on to. Without a constant flow of alcohol into my system, I shook and sweat all the time. My mind raced with desperately confusing thoughts. Nothing felt real, stable, or safe. I screamed to God that I was sick of my life, my family, and my so-called friends. With one shaking hand pointing at ground beneath my feet, I demanded that my life be changed or else He should take me out of the picture once and for all. I had reached the bottom of my pit and had no strength in me to begin the climb upward.

I fell to my knees on the carpet and, in a cracked, bellowing voice, repented for what I had done to my life, to my son, and to everyone I had ever loved. The enraged demands of a few moments before transformed into pleas for forgiveness and salvation. I submitted to God for the second time in my life and asked to be brought out of the darkness I had created around me. With hot tears running down my face, I repented, I asked, and I received Jesus Christ into my fully sincere heart. My way wasn't working; it would kill me if I didn't change.

There were no flashing lights, no angels singing, no miracles, and no immediate end to my pain. Instead, my heartbeat slowly calmed, and the tears began to dry. My cathartic confessions and submission to God left me as a clean slate. I remembered that there was a plan in place; the knots in my soul were being refashioned into a ladder to climb out of the pitch-black pit. Recovery was not going to be easy or painless, but neither was the destructive path I had taken to where I was then.

The outpatient recovery group provided the support, structure, and distraction necessary for me to solidify my sobriety. Thanks to a renewed faith in Christ and the treatment program I had entered, the slow climb out of the pit progressed a little more every day. Schedule and routine were encouraged. My weekly calendar was filled with AA meetings, sessions and activities with the treatment program, and fishing outings. When I found myself alone with nothing to do to occupy my mind, I would read the Bible.

I visited a popular forest called Westonbirt Arboretum with my small treatment group. The purpose for the trip into nature was to help us reconnect with the world, to spend time actually experiencing our surroundings. I could not remember a more beautiful day. The sun on my face, the smell of the fresh clean air, and the rich colors of the scenery all felt new to me. Like a child, I was witnessing these things for what seemed like the first time. Each of us slowly moved through the trees, collecting fallen leaves. The thin, drying leaves were an enriched spectrum of colors: reds, purples, greens, and yellows. I had never studied leaves so closely and marveled at the intricate networks of veins that, before they fell, had carried nutrients from the roots to the foliage. The beautiful complexity of the world filled me with joy and hope. The beginning of my sobriety had been somewhat overwhelming; the experience of emotions not numbed by alcohol was often painful and confusing. Yet, the emotions I felt in that forest were like the light that fills your eyes after a blindfold is removed, intense but wonderful.

A year into my recovery, I was sitting alone in my apartment. The television wasn't on; I wasn't even reading from my Bible. Without warning or intention, a conviction overtook my heart. I had to get baptized. My repentance had been genuine; I had accepted Jesus Christ into my heart and soul, and now it was time to be baptized as a public profession of my faith.

I dressed and made my way to the first church that came to mind when I decided it was time to be baptized. The service was underway when I arrived, so I sat near the back and listened intently. After the service was complete, I introduced myself to the church's pastor. I shared my story with him, where I had come from and where I was trying to go. He asked what had brought me into the church on that particular day, and I expressed that my heart was convicted; it was time for me to be baptized.

What happened next was much different from what I had hoped for and anticipated. The pastor told me I would need to take that up with the next pastor because he was leaving. I was confused and asked the kindly pastor why he was choosing the leave the church. He admitted to me that the members of that church were too set in traditions. They had become too wrapped up in the rules and were too narrow-minded to experience Christ in a modern world.

I returned home defeated and discouraged.

Two of the tools the devil uses to pull you from Christ are distraction and discouragement. That day, I was distracted by the pastor's opinions and discouraged he had not been able to help me with my baptism. That particular church was not where I was meant to be, and I was unsure what I was meant to do next. The Scripture was clear; in order to truly walk with faith, I had to repent and be baptized. My repentance had been a cleansing, eye-opening experience that would mean nothing if I was not baptized. Yet, I knew God would not abandon me. The sureness of the purpose Christ was imparting into my life was not to be cast aside as I had done before. Instead of wallowing in the defeat of walking out of that church without a plan for baptism, I continued to build myself up with the Word.

Alcoholics Anonymous had been one of the catalysts of my recovery and reclamation of my faith. The founding members of the group were Christian men who fully believed that the power and clarity of Christ had the ability to guide addicts from the brink. I found myself disillusioned, though, by the vague and apologetic manner in which God was incorporated into the program.

"A higher power" is the way God is represented in the twelve-step literature. I understood that advertising AA as a Christian organization might alienate some troubled alcoholics who had not yet accepted Jesus Christ. Yet, to be associated with a group so scared of its own convictions, so worried about offending, made me uncomfortable and frustrated. As trust in the Lord defined itself in my heart and mind, I knew I had to leave AA and find a congregation in which to make my spiritual home.

CHAPTER THIRTEEN

But when they shall lead you, and deliver you up,
take no thought beforehand what ye shall speak,
neither do ye premeditate:
but whatsoever shall be given you in that hour,
that speak ye: for it is not ye that speak, but the Holy Ghost.
MARK 13:11

I WAS WATCHING SOME CHRISTIAN program on the television and reading my Bible one night alone in my apartment. The advertisement playing on Revelation TV was promoting a ten-day guided trip of Israel during the Passover celebration, the Feast of Tabernacles. As details of the scenery that would be experienced flashed across the screen, I felt a palpable conviction overtake my heart. When the commercial ended, I jumped from my chair, bursting into a run toward the computer in my bedroom.

I had £1000 in the bank. The trip, travel, and lodging combined, cost £850. That left me with £150 of pocket money and nothing left over for an emergency. Seconds after confirming my reservation, the reality of the situation began to sink in. Without a doubt, my family would think I had lost my mind when they heard of my plans for pilgrimage. The closest to traveling abroad I had ever come was the menial trips back and forth between England and Northern Ireland. My mother, father, and siblings had still not really come to understand the sincerity of my Christian faith. There would be explaining to do and assurances to make. No matter what my loved ones would think of my decision to follow a new path into a war torn and disputed area, I knew it was what I needed to do. The ground Christ walked on, the unchanged horizons that met his gaze, these powerful places were calling to my soul.

I wrote a letter to my family. I quoted meaningful lines from our family history, expressed my love for our private meanings for song lyrics and simple phrases. I tried my best to explain why I was impulsively compelled to travel to Israel and gave small pieces of advice to my siblings in the event I never made it home. I tucked the letter away, not intending to send it unless I absolutely had to. Once the letter was completed, I felt somewhat more at ease with the possible outcomes of my trip to Israel.

The line for the flight to Tel Aviv, Israel, at Heathrow was made up predominantly of older people. Aside from me, the youngest passengers were in their mid-forties. I turned to the woman behind me, and we talked about how this was our first trip to Israel. There was comfort in her newness to this experience, an understanding that there were people going on this trip who were just as nervous and excited as I was.

After a seriously long flight, my fellow pilgrims and I landed in the confusing bustle of Tel Aviv. The procedure of going through customs, showing our passports, and retrieving our luggage was stressful and somewhat confusing. I was aching to get out of that crowded airport, to officially start whatever spiritual adventure was in store for me.

There was a coach waiting to take us from the airport in Tel Aviv to our first accommodations in Tiberius, which was on the Sea of Galilee. Once outside in the desert air, I said something a friend had told me to remind myself of throughout my journey.

"Here I am," I said.

The weight of what I was doing sank in more during the coach ride to Tiberius. Mountains do not change; those that created the horizon around me were the very ones my Lord and

Savior had seen while He walked the earth teaching his disciples. The road signs we passed indicated the closeness of places like Nazareth and Bethlehem. The places I had escaped to while reading my Bible were real. I felt more at home in this foreign place than I ever had England or Northern Ireland.

"Here I am," I repeated, this time with the joyful yet reverent tone the words commanded.

On the second day in Israel, we boarded the coach and went to Yardenit, the beloved and sacred baptismal site located on the Jordan River, a site on the same river where Jesus was baptized and where hundreds of thousands of pilgrims gathered to do the same. Two men stood in the water, taking the arms of person after person and baptizing them in the name of Jesus Christ. Everyone was given a pure white gown to wear before lining up for a turn at cleansing.

I was scared of the water. Since my near death by drowning at the public pool, I had barely ventured more than ankle deep into the lakes where I fished, save one drunken dive from a cliff that ended in frantic embarrassment. The series of successfully immersed and baptized people leaving the water did very little to calm my nerves. A laundry list of questions popped into my head, the most important of which being how I was to get out of the water.

When it was my turn, I approached the men whose entire job was baptizing soul after soul in the sanctified waters of the River Jordan. One grabbed my right arm, the other my left, and before I could get a single question out of my mouth, the baptism was underway.

"You are David," one of the men proclaimed, "you are a mighty man of God, and you shall be a mighty man of God. I baptize you in the name of the ..."

I could not hear the rest of the practiced words because I was pulled under the water. When I was brought back to my feet and ushered in the direction of the exit, the words the man had said to me became clearer.

How did he know my name? My tour group hadn't met the men before getting in line, and I had never said my name to them before they baptized me. The answer to this question was in the sense of purity and purpose I felt as I walked out of the water in my dripping wet gown. The words I had said when I arrived in Israel came back to mind.

"Here I am," I thought.

I was there with God, baptized and born again.

The next several days of the trip were a blur of places I had read about and imagined without ever fully grasping their reality. Over and over again, I was struck by the trueness of the descriptions present in the Bible, the accuracy with which my mind had formed images of them. On our third night, we moved from the Sea of Galilee to our second accommodations in Jerusalem. Against the velvet backdrop of the night sky, I saw broad, glowing red letters on the horizon. The word these letters spelt was *Shalom*. I did not know this was the name of the hotel we were driving to. To me, the city of Jerusalem was welcoming us travelers in its native language. I was reminded again that Israel felt like my home.

While having dinner with members of my group at the Shalom Hotel, I shared my story with about ten other people. AA had been remarkable practice for opening up and sharing without internal shame or fear of reproof. When my testimony was complete, a man in his seventies pulled me aside. He produced a small book from his shirt pocket and handed it to me. It was called "The Power of Proclamation." As he thanked me for my candor, he told me to study the final four pages closely, to read them over and over again until I could recite the words from memory, until they were so ingrained in my thoughts I could repeat them decades later. The pages he directed me to contained lessons on an often-quoted piece of Scripture, Isaiah 54:17. That passage starts with the line "No weapon formed against thee shall prosper." By giving me that pamphlet and showing me that lesson, the man in his seventies was showing me that as long as I had the convictions of Christ with me in my walk, nothing could break me. Alcohol, drugs, women, fear—these things were no more than a paper sword when up against the power of my faith in the Lord.

After dinner, an older retired couple approached me where I stood. They invited me to speak, to share my testimony, in front of a large audience of believers and a television camera broadcasting to the sixty million people in the United Kingdom. I was flabbergasted, flattered, and certain this was an opportunity I could not graciously deny or walk away from. I accepted and was informed where to be for the broadcast, which was two hours away. The small window of preparation time shook me, but not hard enough to balk. I had agreed to speak, and that was exactly what I planned on doing.

I went back to my hotel room and made calls back home, very expensive calls, letting my family know I was going to be on television in two hours. They excitedly promised to watch. After the phone calls were done, I was left in anxious silence. What was I going to say? That question, so hard to answer, awakened the knots inside of me. This time, however, when the ropes began to tighten, I had a knife with which to cut them loose.

Alone in my room, I began to speak a rebellious prayer to God. I told Him I would not, could not, go on television to bare my truths. Unless He leant me some encouragement, some strength in the face of this anxiety, I would not step in front of those cameras. I opened the Bible, which sat stolidly on the bed in front of me. The page I saw when I opened my eyes at the end of my nervous prayer was from the Gospel of Mark—chapter 13 and verse 11, to be exact. In that passage, we are told not to premeditate the words we speak; when we are called upon, the Holy Spirit will direct our words. My eyes read silently as my mouth read aloud, the passage so calming and perfectly suited to my concern. I stopped worrying about what I would say to the audience and the cameras. The Spirit would direct my testimony, give me the right words in the right order.

An hour and a half later, I was standing in front of a room full of expectant faces and the unblinking stare of television cameras. After one more silent prayer I began to speak. I talked about the beauty of Israel, how the name of the place should really be Is-Real because it provided believers and nonbelievers alike a glimpse at the realities of Scripture. From there, I told the story of my bondage to alcohol and self-destruction and how Christ broke me free from that captivity. It was exhilarating and nerve-racking, a moment that inspired me.

A performance on the ninth night, celebrating the Feast of Tabernacles, was the culminating event of my time in Israel. There were 3,000 people crowding the stadium, and I found it hard to concentrate on what was happening on the stage. No matter how hard I tried to focus on the show commemorating the Passover Feast, my thoughts wandered anxiously back to the mass of strangers on all sides of me.

In a moment of fevered praise and prayer, as I listened to the voices of those terrifying people raising and glorifying their faith, I began to feel heat rising in my back. An invisible, smoldering hot spear was piercing the space between my shoulders. When it first started, I dismissed it as the anxiety that had been making my heart race and face sweat. The heat intensified and spread up my back, and I went numb from my knees downward, forcing me to my knees as I prayed. In waves of heat, paralyzing numbness, and short spells of relief, I knelt on the ground. The fear left; anxiety over the crowd and the unexpected fierce inner fire that had overtaken me fled as I clasped my hands together in supplication with Christ. When the fiery heat subsided, I opened my eyes to a new, calm understanding that the people around me were not to be feared but embraced. Reflection on that new perspective opened my eyes to something I had read in the Bible and never truly connected with until then. The passage that echoed in my soul after that night in the stadium theater warns us that first we will be baptized by water, and then by fire.

After that night, I was fully baptized into this new Christian life.

CHAPTER FOURTEEN

And they shall fight against thee;
but they shall not prevail against thee;
for I am with thee,
saith the Lord, to deliver thee.

JEREMIAH 1:19

THE BIBLE WARNS BELIEVERS to expect opposition and persecution. Just as Jesus Christ met with painful rejection, questioning, and judgment, His followers should be prepared to stand strong in the face of these things. This warning became very real in my life soon after returning from my first trip to Israel.

One of the most memorable occurrences of disbelief happened while I was visiting with Harry and Robert. Before long, the conversation turned to religion, specifically my faith and their lack thereof. The friendly conversation blossomed into a debate and then an inquisition. The two of them fired questions at me that I answered calmly, at first. Voices grew louder, and soon we were all standing nose to nose, the two of them aggressively attacking my views and beliefs. I argued fiercely, barely allowing either of them to get a word in edgewise. They were both much larger than I was, but I felt no fear as I defended my position. I was unmovable.

After the argument spun in circles for several minutes, Robert and Harry took a step back and looked at one another incredulously.

"He's going all the way," one of them muttered with a slight laugh and a shrug.

With that, the confrontation was over. I felt powerful and victorious. The Lord had given me the words and strength to stand up to two ardent men on a mission to pull me away from my faith. I was on fire for Jesus, for my walk in the Spirit. While that experience gave me a glimpse of the adversity I would encounter for the rest of my life, it also confirmed my knowledge that the words of Christ in the Holy Bible were the most beautiful and righteous truth.

Aside from the lost souls questioning my faith, I also began to encounter those in need of my help and guidance. Despite not finding a permanent congregation that felt like the community I belonged in, I traveled around to different churches and shared my testimony. This experiment in evangelism, encouraged by the enthusiastic response of those I shared my experience with, gave me the confidence and assuredness I needed to witness one-on-one for those who needed me.

I met a young woman online named Oonagh who lived in my native Northern Ireland. She quickly became a good friend and confidant, someone I could talk with easily without fear of judgment or reproach. Oonagh was also confused, somewhat lost on her journey. Without pushing her, I presented her with my testimony and answered questions she had about the Bible and what it meant to walk with Christ.

Not long after she and I began to forge and solidify our long distance friendship, Oonagh suffered a tragedy. She called me in the middle of the night, at three in the morning, sobbing uncontrollably. I had to hold my phone away from my barely awake head and let her continue her bitterly hard crying until she could speak clearly. It took a long time to make out through her animalistic cries and bellows that her grandfather had passed away. She had so many emotions devastating her all at once. Grief, anger, disbelief. My heart broke for her but I stayed steady, thanks to my belief that God had a plan for Oonagh. This pain was a part of that plan, and I reassured her with that fact. I surprised myself with my ability to comfort Oonagh in her emotional state. The calmness I was able to maintain was given to me thanks to the direction of the Holy Spirit, which I did my best to express to my young friend.

Two days later, on New Year's Eve, I received another call for help from someone I cared for in Northern Ireland. Robert, my cousin and longtime friend, had developed a serious problem with alcohol. He had been checked into a treatment center to get help managing his addiction but had behaved badly enough to be kicked out. That night, he called me from a field where he was lying on the cold ground drunk, incoherent, and belligerent. Robert's relapse had taken control of him, and I was the person he called for help. From another country, it was my responsibility to try to guide Robert to the saving grace God had given to me when I was in a similar position.

With force and boldness, I commanded Robert to get up from the field and start walking in any direction until he could figure out where exactly he was. It was dark, and Robert was disoriented. After wandering through a few streets, Robert found himself in Newry town center. I told him to get off the phone with me and call himself a cab to take him back to the treatment center in Newcastle. I would call ahead of him and try to convince whoever was in charge to allow Robert to rejoin the rehabilitation program.

A long and tense conversation with an exhausted rehab employee ended with the treatment center finally agreeing to take Robert back, as long as he could stay on track and follow the rules. Meanwhile, Robert had called a cab to take him to Newcastle. It was an expensive ride, and the driver was extremely unhappy when Robert revealed he had no money to pay the fare. The driver, who had no sympathy for a drunken man, drove off with Robert still in the backseat. As far as the law was concerned, Robert was somewhat of a thief for not paying the driver for the ride from Newry. The police decided to keep Robert overnight in a cell as punishment and to give him a chance to sober up.

I knew exactly how Robert must have felt sitting in that cell all night. There is a special kind of shame reserved for chastised alcoholics—a shame that shines a bright light onto the shortcomings and fears that drives us to hide in bottles and shot glasses. Through a sleepy haze, Robert was watching that light illuminate all that had gone wrong that lead him to that cell. I prayed for him that night. My prayers were for Christ to give him the strength to find what I had, a foothold in the sober world.

I decided to turn the strength Christ had brought into my life toward the remaining vice I still kept: smoking cigarettes. While in Israel, I had been the only member of my group who would sneak out after a meal for a roll-up. Several times while I was smoking, I would see the people I was traveling with watching me in quiet disbelief. I could not blame them for the distaste they had for my smoking habit. Our bodies are temples of God and should be treated with deference and respect. There was nothing respectful about inhaling burning, toxic smoke.

In March of 2005, I made plans to spend a week with, Ollie, a friend I had made on my Israel trip. She had a home in Burnham-on-Sea, a coastal town in Somerset about thirty miles away from my flat in Peasedown, St. John. I didn't tell any of my friends or family the specifics of where I was headed or that I was taking this time away to quit smoking for good. The possibility of my brothers, cousins, and friends trying to interfere and offer their own advice or judgments seemed strong, so I chose to push ahead without them. As far as my loved ones knew, I was spending a week away with some fellow Christians. This was true enough; Ollie was a dedicated Christian who shared my beliefs. I would return a week later a refreshed and strong non-smoker thanks, in part, to the assistance a few sets of nicotine patches would give me. That was the plan.

With bags packed, I traveled to my friend's house to relax and get rid of the habit I had become ashamed of. Before long, I realized I had forgotten my nicotine patches and was left with a bit of tobacco and roll-up shells as a safety net. The first partial day was tense but, overall, I was handling the lack of cigarettes fine. Ollie and I prayed together, enjoyed relaxed conversation, and I found some comfort in the calmness of the area itself. Simply being away from my usual routine was helping me separate myself from the need to smoke.

Around the time I went to sleep that first night, the nicotine withdrawal symptoms started to sink in. The next morning, I did not feel well. I was sweating but cold, had a lumbering continual headache, and was easily irritated. Ollie encouraged me to go back to bed for a while, which I did. When I woke up the second time, I was in a panic. Paranoia overtook my usual trusting impression of Ollie. She made me something to eat, which I convinced myself was poisoned or spiked. In a kind-hearted effort to distract me into enjoying my time away, Ollie suggested we take a day trip to the village of Cheddar, where the popular cheese was made. I agreed to the trip and did my best to stay functional.

Once we were in Cheddar and browsing a few quaint shops, I became uncomfortable with the people around me. Even having Ollie close at hand made me feel penned in and trapped. I decided to tap into the emergency supply of tobacco I had stashed in my pocket. Outside, I clumsily made myself a roll-up with shaking hands and racing thoughts.

I had to leave.

That was the thought that kept pushing to the front of my mind. This was not a safe place, and I needed to escape. I called Michael, a friend who lived near my apartment, and pleaded with him to come pick me up. I told him to get to Cheddar as quickly as possible, that I was going through hell and needed to be back at my apartment. Michael got to me quicker than I had imagined possible.

I thought that the paranoia and panic would ease off somewhat after I was in Michael's car and on my way back home. That did not happen. Instead, perhaps due to the enclosed space of the front seat and movement of the passing scenery, everything got worse. I turned to Michael and didn't see the familiar face I had expected. My eyes lied to me with a hallucination of

Michael's face devoid of skin. The skinless monster looked evil and reptilian. I quickly moved my gaze back out the window and took a deep breath, praying that Michael would look more normal and less terrifying when I turned back to him.

Thankfully, the hallucination had passed, and my friend's face was real again. We made it back to my apartment, and Michael helped me dispose of the rest of my tobacco and the forgotten nicotine patches. Since I had made it this far without chemical assistance, I was sure I could handle the rest of what lay ahead. In my paranoid and sickly state, I didn't care whether Michael threw the tobacco away or kept it for himself, as long as it was out of my home. The final thing I asked of Michael was that he not let anyone know that I had come home early from my holiday. I knew it was going to be a trying few days as the withdrawal finished running its course. What I needed was privacy and prayer, not the insistence and concern of family or friends. Michael agreed and left me alone with my struggle.

Over the rest of the week, I prayed for the pain and surreal visions to stop. I cried pleas to Christ to take the temptation to smoke away, remove the desire for it from me completely. The worst of the withdrawal symptoms were the hallucinations. As my brain tried to adjust to a sudden lack of cigarettes it created illusions of rats running around my apartment. I could hear the rodent skittering across the floor and feel them brush against my legs or arms as I tried to rest. It was terrifying and infuriating. My rational mind knew that rats were not truly there, but that logic would be overtaken, leaving me confused and overwhelmed.

Then, my prayers were answered. I woke up one morning near the end of the week, and the hallucinations were gone. I felt more myself than I had in days, but without the urge to smoke. I praised God for delivering me from this ordeal in one piece. Never again have I experienced even a passing desire to smoke. Not even after a heavy meal, when I used to crave a smoke the most. This was a true miracle Christ brought into my life, one I am still awed by and grateful for.

CHAPTER FIFTEEN

We are troubled on every side, yet not distressed;
we are perplexed, but not in despair;
Persecuted, but not forsaken;
cast down, but not destroyed.
2 CORINTHIANS 4:8–9

T HE EARLY MONTHS OF 2006 were filled with an unyielding pain throughout my body. Years of hard work, often
involving long hours of difficult labor, had taken a toll on every
weight-bearing piece of me, especially my back and shoulders.
Regular sleep became almost impossible. After one or two hours
of lying in the same position, my muscles would seize and ache
enough that I woke up. I had to call family to my home to cook
for me and clean because standing still was agony. It hurt to
move, and it hurt to stop moving. Every day I prayed for relief.

The idea of being reliant on prescription medications was
an unhappy concept that I refused. Sobriety had been a battle
and now that I had it, I did not want to hand it over to the pain
gripping at my joints. I did my best to reserve the pills for times
when the ache became a distracting pain that hindered my ability to get out of bed or leave my house for days at a time. Even
then, my continual prayer and Bible study often did more for me
than the pills ever could.

In the midst of my struggle with what wound up being pro-
gressive arthritis, my mother was taken to the hospital with lung
problems. I gathered my wits and managed to make it into the

city to visit with her. My duty as her son was to be stolidly by her side. My heart broke when the pain became too intense to handle in a public setting, and I had to leave. I felt like an animal snared in a trap it could not see well enough to escape from.

I wondered often what lesson God was intending for me to learn, what test I was being given, by living with that constant pain.

My brother Walter lived in the house where our dear cousin Buck had passed away. On May 25, a few days before my birthday, he and a friend were sitting around talking. There was no one else in the house at the time; the upstairs bedroom where the death occurred was empty and quiet. Then, a cold chill filled the room, interrupting the conversation happening between Walter and his mate.

My brother half-jokingly said to his friend, "That must be our Buck."

As Walter and his mate shared a tentative laugh at this observation, my brother's mind was taken over by a thought that did not feel like his own.

"Book a trip to Israel for David."

The words came into his head so clearly, but were not of his own mind. He called to share the persistent thought with me. I couldn't believe the words coming through the phone.

"You're going to Israel," he said.

I told him I couldn't afford to go, but he insisted he would pay my way and not expect me to repay the cost. This threw me for a loop. My brother had always taken pride in his ability to get and spend money. It wasn't like him to give handouts or lavish gifts. Walter told me about feeling our cousin's presence in the home and the voice in his mind that told him to get me back to Israel. He had called his wife Julie, who was out shopping at the time, and told her she had to book the trip when she got home.

It was decided. I was heading to Israel for a second time. The trip was with the same tour group I had traveled with before. This time, they were going for the Feast of Pentecost. I would be there from the 30th of May through the 7th of June, which meant planning my absence and leaving in five short days. This trip was going to be much different from the first in many ways. My first experiences in Israel took away the fear of being in a new, foreign place. Now I had a yearning to be there, a familiar understanding of the power Israel had. My soul and heart were better prepared for the wisdom that sacred land had to share. Thanks to Walter's generosity, I was in Israel five days later.

The purpose of my first trip to Israel was to be baptized and reborn. For my second visit to the Holy Land, the Lord set out to humble me and ready me for true forgiveness. Despite opening my heart to Christ, there were still dark corners in my perceptions where hatred, bitterness, and prejudice still lived.

My childhood experiences ingrained in me a livid dislike for Roman Catholics that had never faded, even after years spent living outside of Northern Ireland. There were also very few minorities or immigrants in the neighborhoods I grew up in or the village I had settled into as an adult. While I had no hatred toward different races, I was inherently uncomfortable and closed off to them. Classmates had called me a darkie, a nigger, and other racial slurs for having somewhat tanner skin than their milky complexion. There was a quiet mistrust of different races that had stayed within me ever since those early encounters with racism. That kind of bitterness and resentment stands directly in the way of everything Christ can bring into your life.

When I stepped onto the tour group coach in Israel on the first day of the 2006 trip, God threw me into the deep end and humbled me into letting go of that bitterness. Of the fifty members of the tour group, more than thirty were different races from all over the globe, and almost all of my fellow travelers were either Catholic or had been previously. On that coach, driving through the place I felt God's presence the most palpably, I was confronted with my own caged perceptions.

God was speaking to me through that experience. The words that came into my heart were, "David, you must let go of every bitterness and resentment, and forgive everyone who has ever wronged you—strangers, friends, and family alike. Only then can I forgive you."

It was an intense mandate. The time I spent in Israel getting to know and care for people I never would have met without the power of Christ dismantled the bars around my heart. Resentments and bitterness evaporated, and I was left with peace in my spirit. The presence of God washing over me while I was on the Sea of Galilee was a sign of the blessings that letting go and forgiving would bring to me.

Not once did while walking miles with the tour group did I feel the pain that had haunted me for the previous months. My back and shoulders never wavered, and I was able to take in my surroundings without the distraction of constant pain or prescription tablets. I took countless photos of the sacred sites and monuments. Then, while browsing a gift shop in Bethlehem, I lost my camera. I had set the case down to pay and either left it on the counter, or it was stolen. I was upset at losing my pictures but knew that no still image could truly capture what I felt in Israel, how it feels to have the fearsome but wonderful force of God fill your body and soul with love, light, and pure forgiveness.

Shortly before returning home to England, I met an old married couple who were also from the United Kingdom. I delivered my testimony to them and told them about the time I had spent visiting different churches. I expressed an interest in finding a congregation I could plug in to and be a part of. They were familiar with Bristol and recommended a Baptist church there.

A month after my trip to Israel, I got my driver's license back. I was proud and excited for my fresh freedom. Thanks to the end of my driving ban, I got myself a job driving a large industrial tanker. I had successfully completed the steps the judge had required of me in order to stay out of prison. The judge was adamant that he never wanted to see me again, and I had stayed out of his court room. By earning back the privilege of driving,

I was proving to the world, myself, and Christ our Lord that I was serious and committed to maintaining my sobriety.

I entered a fishing match that August. While fishing, I was able to clear my mind and fully relax. The process of fishing, from baiting the hook to reeling in a catch, required all of my attention. Grander thoughts, concerns, and worries were laid aside for a few hours while I focused on that simple, happy task. For £10 I secured my spot in the competition; the first prize of £25 would go to the fisherman who reeled in the most weight in fish. I very much wanted to win.

The match began at 9:00 a.m. Moments after the whistle blew to signal the official start, I dropped my kit into the water. Then, my line broke, and the pole faltered. It took me thirty minutes to gather my soaking wet kit, reset my line, and cast for the first time. There was no way I could make up for the lost time. The competition was over for me, I thought, so I relaxed and continued fishing as if I were alone in the water. I smiled and enjoyed myself. After several hours, the whistle blew again, and the match was over. More out of curiosity than sport, I brought my haul to be weighed. Much to my surprise, I had won the match with an impressive weight of 74 pounds, 3 ounces. Shocked and grateful, I received my reward and the pride of besting the crowd of older, more experienced men. My grace in the face of an exceptionally frustrating situation felt better than the small cash prize. I thanked God for granting me the inner peace and wisdom needed to relax in that moment of tension.

CHAPTER SIXTEEN

Let the woman learn in silence with all subjection.
But I suffer not a woman to teach,
nor to usurp authority over the man,
but to be in silence.

1 TIMOTHY 2:11–12

I HAD KEPT THE SMALL scrap of paper with the name and address of the church the older English couple had given to me. The location of the church was somewhat concerning to me. Certain parts of Bristol were infamous for crime, drugs, and homeless wanderers. The recommended church happened to be square in the middle of one of those areas. I considered the chances of running into a couple familiar with my area while visiting Israel and decided to give the church a chance. After all, Jesus had come for the common man, the vagrants, and the sinners. On the corner of a dangerous, dingy street may be the ideal place to worship.

The eighteen-mile drive to Bristol did not bother me much, even though I drove past nearly half a dozen churches on my way out of Peasedown, St. John. God had taken me all the way to Israel twice already. A thirty-six mile round trip once a week seemed like an insignificant distance. The first Sunday services I attended created a strong impression. I sat on one of the long, wooden pews. Though I'm not sure what I expected, the highly traditional seating caught me somewhat off guard. I was reminded of my childhood in Northern Ireland and the Baptist church I attended there.

The pastor was a prodigiously tall man in his sixties. The sermons he delivered to the congregation were moving and eloquent; he was a good shepherd of God. As in most churches, the pastor's wife was also very visible and involved with the services. She was nearly his exact opposite, both physically and otherwise. Short of stature but giant in personality, she came off as domineering and bold in her opinions. As the leader of a four-woman worship team, the pastor's wife was at the center of most of the church's events. From what I could see, being in the spotlight was something she enjoyed. Even though I was not offended or shocked by a pastor's wife who reveled in the attention of the congregation, there was something troubling about that woman's behavior.

A typical Sunday service was roughly an hour long. Many times, the pastor delivered a wonderful twenty-to-thirty minute sermon. Then, his wife would address the congregation for the remainder of the time. She lead prayer and directed events as though the congregation belonged to her, not to her husband, the pastor. At first, this did not bother me. Yet, as I read more Scripture and realized how often we are directed that women are meant to learn and worship in silence, I began to be uneasy with the hierarchy of that church.

Moreover, there was a serious social division among the members. Newer members of the church were often left out of conversations or not invited to tea parties and other get-togethers. The women of the worship team, with the pastor's wife at the head, stood as leaders of this kind of behavior. On a cold Sunday evening after service, I understood just how standoffish some of those people could be.

Given the area where the church was located, it wasn't unheard of for young street kids to wander into the church for hot tea and biscuits once prayer was over. In my opinion, whether or not these teenagers were true believers was irrelevant. They came to the church for help and company. Many of them were willing to talk to members of the congregation about Scripture, Christ, or anything else that was brought up to them, as long as they were allowed to stand in the warmth of the church and fill their bellies with a few small snacks. One morning, a few of these kids came in from the cold, and I welcomed them with a smile.

To my disappointment, most of the other members, including the pastor's wife, turned their backs on the group of most likely homeless teenagers. I, not one to follow the crowd no matter my personal thoughts on the matter, stayed with them at the back of the church and told them to fill their pockets with the leftover biscuits. They were a little loud and boisterous but were willing to listen as I delivered my testimony and spoke of my faith.

A few minutes passed, and the other people still in the church were growing progressively uncomfortable about what they perceived as unwelcome interlopers. A man I knew by appearance but not name walked over and began ushering them toward the front door and back into the chilly autumn night. I decided to follow them outside and continue our conversation. One of the young men, barely more than a boy, paid particular attention to my words and prayers. By the end of our talk, he was throwing his arms around me and crying. I did not understand how the rest of the congregation could so easily turn their backs on those kids when their young souls were so obviously in need of Christ's love and direction. The Spirit did not discriminate; all were welcome on the path. Why should they be so cliquey and choosey?

The dominance of the pastor's wife began to trouble me more often. One night, I awoke at three in the morning with a Scripture heavy on my heart. The Bible instructs us in multiple verses across several chapters and books that women are not meant to be in positions of power within the church. Not lesser by any means, women are the support and caregivers to their husbands. Men who are touched by Christ, charged by God, and moved by the Spirit are who should be at the head of the church delivering sermons.

God wanted me to show that woman the Scripture. She had to know. I knew I had no control over her, no say-so in the church. Yet, I also knew I wouldn't sleep well until I took the step of bringing my thoughts and conviction to her attention. First, I would call the pastor and get his thoughts. Perhaps he could give me some insight on how to handle the situation.

The next morning, I called the pastor. After explaining how

God had awoken me in the early morning hours with that Scripture for his wife and what I felt that Scripture related to, I was surprised to hear him chuckle and sigh. He said if I approached his wife with that passage and my opinions, I was a better man than him. The pastor understood my position and agreed that the biblical instructions regarding women in the church were quite clear. There were no veiled parables, no metaphoric anecdotes, just simple rules we are meant to follow. Sometimes, the Bible makes it very easy to understand the lesson being taught, and this was one of those occasions.

The Sunday after that divine inspiration, I waited while most everyone filtered to the back of the church and left. When the crowd had thinned, I turned and walked toward the pastor and his wife, who were moving back up the aisle to the front. She was in the lead, her towering spouse behind her.

"God woke me with a Scripture for you," I said to her when we had reached each other.

She smiled, glowing in the spotlight of a Bible passage selected especially for her. The smile faded when I pointed out the verse from 1 Timothy, and a bulldog-like grimace took its place. Her response was more volatile than I had expected.

"I do not agree with that!" she yelled, pointing an aggressive finger at the Bible and waving her other arm at her side.

Shock and frustration filled me from toes to scalp.

"Well," I said in a low and calm voice, "that's God's Word."

The Bible contained the truths of the world, words chosen by our Lord to guide us on our journey. To pick and choose which parts suited you and which you ignored was to disrespect that sacred text. My eyes turned to her husband, still standing behind her, who could do nothing but turn his palms to the heavens and roll his eyes in defeat.

It was as though he was silently saying to me, "She is my wife, what would you have me do?"

I walked out of the church in the tough part of Bristol that day and never went back. Even though that congregation had not been the one I could truly plug into, I had learned a valuable lesson about myself over the seven months I spent there. Truth meant more than social acceptance; an honest walk with Christ was to be valued above being embraced by strangers. I had learned from Christ that you can tell a tree by its fruit. A rotten tree is only able to produce rotten fruit, while a healthy tree produces the succulent and beautiful fruit we can thrive on. Is it the tree's fault that it is rotten, or is it the fault of those who tend its roots?

I knew leaving that church was the right decision, but I felt unsatisfied with the way that it ended with the pastor's wife. For several weeks I prayed, asking God to guide me. I knew that leaving would do nothing to change what was going on, and not just in that particular church. Something inside of me knew that many churches all over the United Kingdom were picking and choosing which Scriptures they wanted to adhere to.

When the answer came to me, it seemed so obvious. I would get in touch with the bishop of Bristol. As the head of the city's churches, he would know how to go about remedying the illness of selective observance of God's law. My constant prayer confirmed that I needed to get in touch with the bishop and bring this to his attention. He was a very busy man with many responsibilities. I thought he would appreciate my input into a problem he had overlooked.

I started by trying to call and email his office. My phone calls were either unanswered, or his secretary received them.

"The bishop is busy," she would say one week.

"The bishop has left for a holiday," she would say another.

I tried to stay optimistic yet dogged in my attempts to contact the bishop. God had given me this task; that was clear to me. Giving up, shrugging my shoulders, and going back to my search for a church to get involved with was not an option. If I kept calling, the bishop would eventually need to listen to me.

It took almost two months. Either the bishop suddenly became much less busy, or he and his secretary realized I wasn't going away. He called, and we arranged to meet at a café near a church in Bath he was visiting. I would bring my Bible with the

Scriptures I had been studying, and he would hear what I had to say, of that much I was certain.

The night before the meeting, I prayed for the Lord to empower me with the strength and wisdom I would need to convince the bishop of the changes I believed needed to be made in the churches of Bristol. At around two in the morning, I woke up with a drive to go to my Bible. As always, I said a prayer and then opened the Book to where I was being guided. What I found was a section of verses dealing with the role of leaders in the church and the temptation power can present to those leaders. God had given me these Scriptures for the bishop; these were passages he needed to see. I made note of the Scriptures and went back to bed feeling fully prepared for the impending meeting.

I arrived at the café before the bishop, who joined me shortly after the agreed upon meeting time. After quick introductions, thanks, and obligatory handshakes, I told the bishop the details of my experience at the Baptist church. He listened politely. Nodding, smiling, or frowning in all the appropriate places. I showed him the Scripture God had placed on my heart for him in the middle of the night and expressed my troubling concerns for how the edicts of the Bible were being neglected by the church I had just left, and possibly many other congregations in the United Kingdom.

When I had finished speaking my piece, the bishop remained quiet for a moment. The weight of my words seemed to sink into him as he sat there formulating a response.

"David," he finally said, "you are just like my friend. He is an evangelist. I agree with you, but you have to understand my hands are tied. Those above me set the orders for the churches of Bristol. My job is to carry out those orders."

He conveyed regret that there wasn't more he could do for me but promised to bring these issues and worries to the men in power above him, the men who could enact real change. The bishop all but promised to move mountains in support of my cause, and I felt understood by this important and powerful man. The final promise he made was to keep me apprised of his progress on this matter, saying that he would contact me soon with a hopefully positive update. I left that café in Bath satisfied and anxious to hear from him again.

The bishop of Bristol never called or emailed me again. Though this was disappointing and frustrating, there was little I could do at that point. My role was complete. I had done all I could to set right what had gone off track in the church. It was time to continue my search for a church, a congregation, I could really plug in to.

While I was attending church in Bristol, I had met a woman from London who had stopped by one Sunday service to pray while she was visiting the city. The church was nearly empty after the sermon, and socializing had completed that evening. The woman sat alone on a pew, and it looked as though she had been crying. I approached her, wanting to offer comfort.

The older woman and I spoke at length about her family, my testimony, and the importance of the church community. She informed me that she belonged to a group in London called the UCKG, which stood for the Universal Church of the Kingdom of God. When she shared with me the details of the churches, called "help centers," and the impassioned young ministers, the sadness on her face melted away. It was obvious that the UCKG represented a source of happiness and strength in her life. I was intrigued immediately.

There was a UCKG help center in Cardiff, Wales; a sixty-mile train ride away from my home in Peasedown. I would spend an entire day away from home in order to attend the Sunday meetings at the help center, but the woman from London had given me the impression it was worthwhile. Christ had placed that woman on my path to direct me to the UCKG. I prayed, asking God if the UCKG was where He wanted me to turn next. My prayers were answered by a sense of surety and calm determination that the choice had already been made. I would find out what the help center was all about and what it had to teach me.

My first experiences at the UCKG help center in Cardiff were unique and exhilarating. The young South American preachers were bold and hard hitting. I had never experienced such energetic sermons. Prayers and hands rose in the crowd as the preachers stirred the Holy Spirit in all of us to almost uncontrollable levels. I felt connected to Christ's presence in a way I hadn't experienced since I was in Israel. It was a beautiful gift those preachers had, to connect those in attendance at the help center with the awe-inspiring power of God. After the service, volunteers would take to the streets of Cardiff, handing out pamphlets and encouraging conversation on Scripture, faith, and the mission of the UCKG to anyone who would stop long enough to listen. My inner evangelist reveled in the opportunity to enlighten unbelievers and share my testimony. The deep passion I had for people, especially those society doesn't care about, was reinforced by the hours I spent speaking to strangers around the help center.

During one of those fevered sermons, I was touched by the Spirit. Just as I had experienced in the auditorium and on the Sea of Galilee in Israel, my body got uncomfortably hot, and waves of electrified tingles washed over my body. From the top of my scalp to the bottoms of my feet, God filled my body with loving light. I walked out of the center that day feeling better than any drink had ever made me feel, more loved than any random woman ever could.

Not every day spent at the UCKG ended with such fulfilling emotions, however. Built in to the services were pitches for products like anointed oils designed to add potency to prayer or healing. The preachers encouraged the congregation to purchase these items or donate directly to the church. If you neglected to do so, a heavy guilt replaced the resplendent joy of connecting with the Spirit through worship. I was troubled by these young preachers, so blessed and gifted, who chose to use what God had given to them as a way to take money from believers. It left me with a bad taste in my mouth and disquiet in my soul.

UCKG was not the church for me, but the experience of ministering to strangers on the street ignited the fire within me to speak out about the path of Christ to anyone who cared to listen.

CHAPTER SEVENTEEN

But the God of all grace,
who hath called us unto his eternal glory by Christ Jesus,
after that ye have suffered a while,
make you perfect, stablish, strengthen, settle you.
To him be glory and dominion for ever and ever. Amen.
1 Peter 5:10–11

I GOT MY JOB BACK, collecting refuse bins for the council. The same office that had fired me for missing more than thirty Monday shifts due to raging hangovers had received recommendations in favor of my rehiring, and I was taken back on. My body had aged and ached from the hard labor, but I was proud to be doing this work again. Even the soreness in my ankles and back was a part of the beautiful clarity I had found.

A balance was necessary, a sign of my thanks to Christ for the blessings I had been given. For the first time in my life, I donated blood. Though somewhat scary and uncomfortable, giving blood filled me with excited joy. Alcoholics and drug addicts aren't allowed to give blood; it was incredible to know my blood was clean and pure, worthy of helping someone. My blood would save a life. Unless you have been in a place where destroying your health was a daily activity, you cannot truly understand the triumph found in donating a part of yourself to aid in the healing of another.

Donating blood also made me feel more connected with those I prayed for. Every two weeks, a street pastor I had met years before mailed me a list of the names of people in need of assistance through prayer, a voluntary role known as intercessor.

The friend who introduced me to intercession spent time preaching on the street, using watercolor paintings of biblical scenes to draw in passersby. Children would see the colorful pictures being created before their eyes and insist their parents bring them over to watch more closely. This would lead to the parents speaking with the pastor about the stories being told by the paints and the Christian teachings they represented. He wasn't aggressive or judgmental, just a smiling man of faith sharing his talent for preaching and painting with the world. I was inspired by his quieter brand of evangelism. When he asked if he could send me a list of people to pray for, I accepted without hesitation. The twenty minutes spent asking God to touch the lives of the people on my list had the potential to make an impact that would be felt for years.

I was an intercessor for over a year and a half when I received an interesting offer from the head of the painting pastor's prayer and ministering group. He called me at home and said God had laid me on his heart for a role in his street ministry, delivering my testimony. I agreed readily once again, sure this testimony delivery would be similar to the others I had participated in at several churches. Plus, I believed that nothing could be more nerve-racking than standing in front of television cameras in Israel. We made plans for me to meet him at the Manver Street Baptist Church in Bath.

My expectation of an easygoing outing to give my testimony was quickly dispelled. The warm July weather had drawn what seemed like all of England to Bath. I found myself in the outdoor city center, holding a microphone as hundreds of weekend shoppers and tourists milled around me on all sides. God had tossed me into the deep end again, with just enough ground at my feet to keep my head above water. I closed my eyes briefly and reminded myself that I had told this story before; these words were directed by the Holy Spirit. The details of my walk with Christ easily flowed from my lips in an emphatic yet calm voice. There was strength in those words, and I let go of the nervousness brought on by the crowd. The bishop of Bristol had called me an evangelist, my cousin said the same in jest a few years before, and I was beginning to believe they were correct.

Another call came soon after the day I spent in Bath's city center. The man who ran the street ministry in Bath told me about the small hall he was planning to rent below the YMCA in Bath for two Wednesday evenings. The plan was to invite people in from the street to hear testimony and pray together. He invited me to stop by and share my story once more. The gathering was an excellent chance for me to reach out to the troubled souls I connected and identified with. Even if people came only for a cup of hot tea and a handful of biscuits, the words of praise and belief would still surround them as they sat with us.

I arrived at the hall a few minutes past the official eight o'clock start time. When I came in, there were already five or six people sitting and talking quietly. The man who had invited me saw me enter the hall and smiled broadly.

"Ah, here's David," he said in a loud and cheery voice. "Go ahead, do your stuff."

No time to meet the other people, take a breath, or make a cup of tea. As quick as I could walk to the front, I was reciting the details of my personal testimony. I had been tossed back into the deep end by God, but there was no fear. There was only the peaceful joy of proclaiming the glory of God, the power walking with Christ has to transform and bless a man in his darkest hours. The words came easily that time, and I felt good about the part I played. That first meeting was successful enough to inspire those renting the hall to extend the lease for as long as people were interested in coming. Though my job with the council left me exhausted, I committed myself to minister with the group. It was good work, work that had to be done.

My connections with that group brought me to the street pastor program. The members of the program patrolled the pubs and night clubs in Bath on Friday and Saturday nights. Street pastors would be there as a listening ear, helping hand, and sober voice of reason for the kids hopping from one bar to the next. On August 2, 2008, I went and applied to join the program. Acceptance would mean leaving work Friday evening, taking just enough time to shower and eat dinner, and then walking miles on the streets of Bath until 3:00 a.m. on Saturday.

At first, I was unsure how the bouncers and business owners would feel about and react to the street pastors. Even though we were there to help, I thought it was possible for outsiders to see our actions as interfering with their business. My past experiences with bouncers, in my old ways, had been jarring and sometimes violent. On my first night on the streets with my patrolling partner, those worries were disproved. The bouncers appreciated our ability to keep potentially raucous situations from escalating, and the business owners knew that safe customers were better than injured, arrested, or scared-off customers. We were often welcomed in to the pubs we stood outside of, offered free soft drinks, and allowed to pass out flyers and placards.

Years before, I had been one of those tottering, drunken kids meandering from one bar to the next. It was a privilege to be there to protect them from quandaries similar to those I found myself in while I was drinking and partying. The walking was torture on my arthritic joints, the time as much the same on the rest of me. I persisted through the pain and exhaustion, sure that my faith and the rewards of the work would renew my body as well as my spirit.

Sometimes, it was as simple as clearing broken glass from the sidewalks so people wouldn't get hurt. Other times, my fellow street pastors and I had to serve as physical barriers to break up a fistfight. I counseled crying girls whose boyfriends had abandoned them, helped intoxicated boys find their way into a cab, and talked arguing couples away from resorting to blows. Every Saturday was its own adventure with one main detail in common. I spent time talking to every person I met about the glory of God.

My mother was ill. She had lung issues that were slowly yet surely taking her breath and leaving her weakened. I spent as much time as I could by her side in support and prayer. Every time I had to leave her side was difficult, just as it had been the previous time she was hospitalized with breathing issues. The first time I had needed to leave her, it had been my own pain taking me away. This time, I was needed elsewhere doing God's work and earning my paycheck. Even though I knew my reasons for taking time away from my ailing mother were justified, it still broke my heart. It was clear to me and my siblings that our mother was not long for this world, no matter how hard she fought to keep going. I wanted to spend as much time as possible with her as the sober, strong, faithful man I had become.

I sat with her, remembering the fiercely strong woman she had been before time and illness had weakened her tiny frame, reciting prayers, and declaring my love for her. There would be no regrets when the Lord took her spirit home, nothing I wished I had said. The time by my mother's side would be a blessing well spent.

CHAPTER EIGHTEEN

Blessed be God, even the Father of our Lord Jesus Christ,
the Father of mercies,
and the God of all comfort;
Who comforteth us in all our tribulation,
that we may be able to comfort them which are in any trouble,
by the comfort wherewith we ourselves
are comforted of God.

2 Corinthians 1:3–4

M Y BODY WAS WEARING down.
I had prayed for my job back on the council, thought it would be a chance to redeem myself and feel active. That prayer had been answered and for that, I was grateful. I had not anticipated the strain such activity would put on me. We are always younger in our minds than we are in our bodies. I had no intention of giving up in the face of a challenge, plus the money the job brought in was needed. To compensate, I took a smaller role with the street pastors program, which replaced miles of walking each weekend with a position that called for sitting and more regular hours. I also took to carefully wrapping my right ankle, which helped with hauling over a thousand bins each shift. The days were still busy, barely leaving me time to eat and sleep, but they were far less painful.

Despite the aches and weariness, I was content. There was peace in my soul, peace that made it easier to cope with seeing my mother lying sick in a hospital bed. I believe the fullness of my schedule also made that a less daunting task. While with her, I could be as strong for her as I had to be. I tried to make her smile, help take her mind off the slow suffocation she was enduring. When I left her side, there was other work to be done that kept me from worrying about her.

Then in December of 2008, after five months on the job, a troubling new medical problem took over my life. My stomach blew up to the size of a pregnant woman. Going to the bathroom became difficult, and I was in pain worse than any sore ankle, shoulder, or hangover. I missed work, going back and forth to the hospital for tests and prescriptions. A month passed with no change in my condition, and my mood began to suffer. The doctors surmised the problem with my stomach was due to the poor eating habits I had developed over the past months spent working, ministering, and traveling hundreds of miles each week to do so. Yet, they were having trouble figuring out a solution. The medical treatments became increasingly humiliating, as scans and blood tests became colonoscopies and enemas. I was beginning to feel like an old man, a helpless invalid. Just as I was finding a happy stride in a life with direction, it was taken back and replaced with a swollen gut and demeaning doctor visits. Though I trusted the wisdom of God and was grateful for the tests and lessons He had for me, human patience had limitations.

In February there was still no real answer. I went back to the hospital to have cameras inserted, once again, to study my insides. I was put under partial anesthesia that, I was told, would keep me from feeling the pain of the procedures. The pain was still there, however, and I woke up after the test was done with foggy memories of screaming without hearing my voice. That vague recollection of the soundless pleas for mercy was worse than the months of tests, the painful bloating, and the missed work combined.

The tortuous cameras did yield a result. Years of neglected health in my youth and the poor diet I had been keeping over the recent months had resulted in a buildup of acid in my stomach and esophagus. I was put on a daily medication that I would need to take for the rest of my life. Such a small solution, that pill, which solved such a massive issue in my life. The true answer wasn't in the medication, though, but in the healing power of my faith. The glory of my recovery was owed to God. By the end of April, I was back at work. The proportions of my stomach returned to normal, and I was able to resume a somewhat normal life.

My progress back toward normalcy after the health issues had abated ended abruptly that May. Mrs. Grace Smalley, the matriarch of our family, lost her battle with emphysema. I wasn't with her when she passed. I had left the hospital in Bath where she was being treated only an hour before she died. My sister Tracy and several other family members were with her in the end. One of my brothers called to give me the news. My mother had looked serene, he said, and her final breaths were painless. In a way, there was joy knowing she would no longer be struggling for each bit of air she took in, no longer confined to a bed. She had gone Home.

My brothers, sister, and I began preparations for my mother's memorials. There had to be two funerals held. Since moving to England, my mother had become a beloved personality in Radstock, where she and her second husband Larry had settled and operated their pub. England was where her children, grandchildren, and dearest friends had made their lives. Though her final wishes indicated that she wanted to be buried back in Northern Ireland, it would be unfair to deprive her friends and loved ones in England the chance to honor her. She was a little lady, but she commanded armies.

We placed a lock of her hair, photographs, and keepsakes into a wooden box that would be buried beneath a headstone for her in England. As the eldest son, it was my obligation and privilege to stand up and speak. I recited her favorite poem, *Wit's End Corner*, and the passage from Scripture she often quoted when giving advice to us when we were distressed.

"Let not your heart be troubled," she would say, which referred to John 14:1–6. When she said those words to us, a bit of her strength poured over, and we were able to stand firm in whatever situation was causing us grief. The same Scripture was to be placed on her headstone in Northern Ireland.

I was apprehensive when I approached my siblings with the passage, unsure if they would understand its importance and accept God's words as our mother's epitaph. They quelled my worry quickly, though. All of them agreed the passage was perfect, a beautiful testament to what our mother would say if she could speak to her grieving children. The knowledge of her painless rest and my faith that God stood there with me as I spoke allowed me to deliver a passionate and complete speech about the woman who had brought me into the world and stood by my side through my darkest hours.

After the service in England, we brought our mother back to Northern Ireland. The second burial would take place at a St. Margaret's Church in Downpatrick, the same church where I had married the mother of my dear son. Unlike the first memorial, my family and I planned a full wake and funeral. My brothers put the details together with the pastor of the church; my job was limited to delivering the eulogy.

Just as we had in England, my family gathered to say goodbye to Grace and celebrate the vibrancy of her long life. This time, we lined up to see her in the coffin that had been so lovingly chosen for her to bid her spirit farewell from this world and blissful respite in the next. After the readings, blessings, and goodbyes were all said, our mother was buried beneath a second headstone with the chosen Bible verse inscribed onto it.

"Let not your hearts be troubled," I could almost hear her saying to us as we cried together by her grave.

CHAPTER NINETEEN

For the Lord God is a sun and shield:
the Lord will give grace and glory:
no good thing will he withhold from them that walk uprightly.
O Lord of hosts, blessed is the man that trusteth in thee.

PSALMS 84:11–12

WHILE ATTENDING ONE OF the meetings in the hall above the YMCA in Bath months before my mother's death, I had made a friend named Michael. On the night of the third or fourth meeting, he sat across the table from me, an older man with kind eyes.

"David," he called across the table, "do you mind if I come sit by you?"

I invited him to take the empty chair next to me. There was a sadness mixed in with his agreeable demeanor. His poignant thoughts on Christ and Scripture made him endearing. More than the childhood lesson of respecting one's elders, I had affection and a kind of reverence for Michael almost immediately. As the weeks passed and we started spending more time together outside of the meetings, I realized he was lonesome and in need of the friendship I had to offer him. He had a history of psychiatric issues and an eccentric personality that pushed most people away. Aside from his cats and the gentle parishioners who put up with him, there was no one in his life to care for him.

Weekly meetings increased to seeing him three to four times a week. I learned about the passion he had for his quiet but insistent faith. Michael had a skill I had not yet mastered, that being the ability to express myself forcefully while remaining harmless and allowing others to speak more often than I did. I learned from him in the time we spent together, but I also felt the responsibility of having Michael latch on to me for support and friendship.

Michael and I talked a lot about my two trips to Israel, especially my baptism in the River Jordan. Already in his sixties, Michael hadn't been to Israel and was concerned he wouldn't have a chance to go before he passed away. About a year into our friendship, Michael asked me if I would go to Israel with him. Though I felt bad disappointing him, I answered that I didn't have the funds to make another trip to Israel, as I hadn't been able to work regularly. That did not stop Michael, though, who immediately offered to pay me to be his traveling companion. This caught me entirely off guard. I did not expect Michael to make such a generous offer. It was clear to me that my friend was extremely committed to making the pilgrimage and did not plan to go alone.

I was touched by Michael's offer but told him I did not want to feel indebted to a friend, especially a new friend. He shrugged my refusal off and insisted I think it over. He looked at me with the big sad eyes that often got him his way. I told him I would think it over, pray about it, and get back to him soon with my final answer. Prayer would help me figure out whether my first instincts were indeed correct or I should agree to accompany Michael to the Holy Land.

Once alone in my quiet apartment, I retrieved my Bible and set myself to prayer. The conversation with God and my request for guidance put everything into clear perspective. It had been my own pride that refused Michael's offer, my unwillingness to accept charity. I realized that what Michael proposed was not a handout; it was a mutually beneficial arrangement. Michael was a good man of faith who deserved to see all that Israel was and to experience the power of that incredible place. Obviously, there was more for me to do there, as well, or the opportunity to make a third trip wouldn't have presented itself to me. The path was clear, and I could not let my pride block the way. God was using Michael to bless me with a trip to Israel, but He was also using me as a way of blessing Michael with a way to make a pilgrimage to the Holy Land that he would never have made alone. Michael was elated when I agreed to go with him to Israel. The plans were made quickly and, just a few weeks after I returned from my mother's funeral in Northern Ireland, we left for Israel. The opportunity to see Israel through Michael's eyes as we experienced its power was unbelievable. I remembered my own first trip to Israel, the profound and life-altering effects it had on me and the sense of homecoming it brought to my soul. In a way, going with Michael in 2009 was like getting to feel all of those things for the first time again.

The most important part of the trip was the baptismal outing in the River Jordan. Michael was to be cleansed in the waters where I had been, so close to the baptism site of Jesus Christ. At first, I was only going to be there as support and a celebratory friend for Michael. Then, the wife of the producer for Revelation TV, who had gotten me to deliver my testimony on television back in 2004, gave me a truly incredible chance to take part in the baptisms myself.

"You are over-qualified to assist with the baptisms," she said to me when I tried to refuse graciously.

When asked to stand in the River Jordan and participate in twenty-six baptisms, though, I knew I could not walk away. God had provided this opportunity along every step of this trip, from Michael offering to pay my way to the TV producer's wife making the suggestion.

The fear of water I had held onto since childhood never occurred to me as I stood in the constant motion of the river. Not once did my mind trouble me with concerns of losing my footing and being swept under the water. There was only the connection I felt with Christ and the important work of assisting in each of the twenty-six baptisms I was present for, including Michael's. Five years before, I had been the one being baptized unto Christ in the waters. It was then that my second chance had been granted, my fresh start in a new life. To come so far in that half a decade that I was reciting prayer and holding the weight of strangers as they took that same first step in their own faithful walk was nothing short of a miraculous blessing.

We went to the Dead Sea with the tour group. There was a tradition of covering your body with mud from the river and then floating in the heavily salted water. The mud and the water were said to have healing, restorative qualities unlike any spa treatment found anywhere else on the planet.

Aside from my baptism in the River Jordan, I hadn't done more than wade ankle deep into still waters to fish since nearly drowning at the age of ten. To relax and float in foreign water seemed impossible to me, at first. Then, I remembered where I was. Israel was my spiritual home, the safest place for both my soul and my body. In Israel, I felt no pain, thanks to the strengthening presence of God. With that in mind, I joined my fellow pilgrims in the mud and then the water.

It took me a couple of tries to float, to make my muscles stop tensing up and allow myself to be supported by the salty Dead Sea. To some people, floating in a few inches of water with hundreds of other people may seem like a small thing. To me, however, it was a huge thing, a victory of great magnitude. I was slowly walking up a staircase toward heaven, each step cobbled with more blessings than the last.

Sadness, grief, and physical pain left my body as Michael and I toured Israel together. The historic and religious monuments were the same as they had been the first and second time I had visited, but to Michael they were fresh and new. The physical proof of the stories in the Bible towered around us, all at once humbling, inspiring, and empowering us. Michael was calm, aglow with happiness and excitement. What I found remarkable was the number of small animals, cats primarily, who wandered up to Michael for a pat on the head. In a country where military men can be seen carrying guns in front of sacred buildings, my traveling companion attracted the smallest and most helpless residents of Israel to his feet.

CHAPTER TWENTY

For I am not ashamed of the gospel of Christ:
for it is the power of God unto salvation to every one that believeth;
to the Jew first, and also to the Greek.
For therein is the righteousness of God revealed from faith to faith:
as it is written,
The just shall live by faith.
ROMANS 1:16–17

I HAD MADE A FRIEND in Israel named Edna who lived in London with her family. She was a faithful, educated woman who found immense joy in sharing Christian knowledge with the people she knew. Over the four years since we had first met, Edna had sent me pamphlets containing a wealth of information and interpretations of Scripture. We are living, breathing letters to the world about the teachings of Christ and the laws of God. Much like the letters from the apostles that make up so much of the Bible, our living letters can be used to teach and inspire others. Not to condemn, convict, convert, or convince anyone, but to provide an example of the blessings a true and dedicated life of faith can provide.

The Holy Spirit, over time, convicted my heart to seek out a church that would give me a community of believers to plug into. In many of the small books and pamphlets Edna sent me, a particular church was mentioned that intrigued me. I wanted to know more. There was a sense of urgency, a need for confirmation that this church might indeed be the next step in my journey with Christ.

In the midst of my time spent praying and studying Scripture, I received a call from Edna, who was highly skilled at listening. A conversation with Edna always gave me clarity and perspective. Her response to my questions was very helpful and enlightening, which made my decision an easy one to make. Simply put, the church I was considering kept the Sabbath as God intends and as the Bible teaches. I would visit a specific church near my home in Peasedown, St. John.

Around Christmas, as my mission to find a church family was taking shape, I reached out to Michael. After returning from my third trip to Israel, I had separated myself somewhat from my friendship with him. I had been unprepared for the obligations that came with spending time with him. Outings once or twice a week to church services, grocery stores, and restaurants evolved into almost daily trips and phone calls. I understood why Michael needed me so often, and he held a special place in my heart, but I had felt an approaching crossroads in my life. I needed more time alone with my thoughts and prayers, which meant creating distance from Michael.

As time passed and I thought more deeply about this new church, I missed him and was curious what he would say about my recent discoveries. I expected him to be upset, or at least standoffish, at the distance I had put between us. He surprised me, though, by answering my call with an upbeat and cheery greeting. After a quick exchange of small talk, I brought up my desire to find a new church, hopefully one in Bath. Michael, who had taken the time to personally visit many of the Christian churches in Bath, told me how much he enjoyed the one I was planning to visit.

That made two people who meant a lot to me who stood behind this new church. God uses the people in our lives to reveal His will, the truth of His words, and the lessons He has to teach. This instance of His influence could not be overlooked or cast aside. I agreed to attend the next service with Michael.

I felt at home at that church in Bath almost immediately. Attending that church was the way it was meant to be. That quick comfort encouraged my focus and invigorated my devotion to following the laws present in Scripture. Glorifying God had brought me more blessings than I could have anticipated. It was my duty to live my life according to the instruction and guidance of God's Holy Bible.

The pastor of my new regular church had a calm and loving tone to his ministry that made me comfortable as a part of the congregation. He was attentive and made a point of introducing himself to me not long after I began taking part in the services.

"If God places you on my heart," he said during one of our initial conversations, "I'll come out and see you for Bible study."

That was the first time since I had begun my quest for the right Christian community within a church that a leader of the church had reached out to me so readily. Even if the pastor never came to my home to read and discuss Scripture together, his offer was so obviously genuine. To me, this was a sign that I was exactly where I was meant to be.

Soon after, God brought me a test instead of a blessing.

My dad called to invite me to his birthday party. He and I hadn't been in regular communication for over eleven years, and his birthday party represented a chance for me to get him back into my life, the new life I had structured around God, His Son Jesus Christ, Scripture, and faith.

The party was going to be on a Saturday night. Not only would attending the birthday get-together put me in a position surrounded by drinking, smoking, and temptation, but it would also mean breaking the Sabbath. I explained to my dad that I wouldn't be able to make it due to my commitment to the Sabbath and my involvement with my new church community.

"If you don't come," he said in an exacerbated and surprisingly angry tone, "then I'll cut you out of my life completely."

He hung up on me after that. I was hurt and shocked that my dad would extend reconciliation to me only to snatch it back at the first sign of not getting his way. In my life, a party did not take priority over God, and I was hoping my dad would respect that. Out of respect, celebration, and honor for the man who had reared me, I sent a card for his birthday with another apology for not going to his party, but I never heard back. After some time had passed, I thought his disappointment over my missing the party would have calmed. I sent a message to him about a Bible I had purchased for him as a birthday gift. My dad did not get in touch with me himself when he received this message but instead gave a response to someone else to deliver to me. He refused the Bible.

I had chosen God over my earthly family, my Father over my dad. The Bible warns the faithful that their greatest detractors and enemies will come from their own households and that we need to trust our heavenly Father to give us the strength to continue to love our families in the face of challenges to our convictions. We are made in God's image, yet His way of thinking is not our way of thinking. God's love is never ending and unconditional, a perfect and boundless love. As instruments in God's hands, we shine forth the light of that love. It is every believer's hope, as it is God's, that all of our loved ones develop a personal and intimate relationship with our heavenly Father. Even though it stung to think my dad would probably never accept me and my beliefs, that pain was alleviated by the knowledge that God is in control and working on my dad's heart as He is continually working on mine.

It would be exactly two years before I was successful in giving my father an inscribed copy of the King James Bible. The connection would be mended, pride and stubbornness set aside, and an understanding reached by God's grace and love.

Faith is often its own reward, providing stability and the knowledge that God is the one in control, that all we need to do is pray. Give thanks and ask God to be present in your life, in both good times and bad. True, unshakeable faith also brings blessings into your life beyond anything you could dream.

One of these blessings was a growing relationship with my son. Gary and I didn't see each other very often, but we exchanged texts and phone calls on a regular basis. One of those calls brought incredible news. My son was going to be a dad; I was going to be a granddad. When Gary told me about the impending birth of his first child, my heart filled with pride, excitement, and joy. There was also an almost overwhelming sense of gratitude. I was grateful to God for my sobriety, the second chance I had been given to be a present and positive influence in the lives of those I loved, and for the opportunity to be a part of a new life being brought into the world. On October 18, 2011, my remarkable grandson, Adam Benjamin, was born.

God brought me and my testimony to the public once again. I was offered two opportunities: to speak in front of a church service about my journey with Christ, and to take part in a radio program in Bristol. I had complete trust in the wisdom of God and His ability to bring me the right words at the right times. The boldness I had once only been able to find in the bottom of a bottle was now fueled by the light of God's glory. My voice spoke strongly with the conviction of faith and the certainty of truths revealed in God's Holy Word. I thanked God for these chances to be heard, to have the potential to touch just a single lost soul and bring them to Christ with the repentance and awe that I had for God's power.

CHAPTER TWENTY-ONE

Make a joyful noise unto the Lord, all ye lands.
Serve the Lord with gladness:
come before his presence with singing.
Know ye that the Lord he is God:
it is he that hath made us, and not we ourselves;
we are his people, and the sheep of his pasture.
Enter into his gates with thanksgiving,
and into his courts with praise:
be thankful unto him, and bless his name.
For the Lord is good; his mercy is everlasting;
and his truth endureth to all generations.
PSALMS 100

M Y LIFE HAD PURPOSE and direction, but there was still something missing. When I was first born again, I prayed that God's plan for me would include a woman I could marry and build a life with. In my heart, I knew a partner and a child would bring completeness to my life that my faith in God had prepared me to achieve.

In order to receive the blessings God has in store for us, we sometimes need to take action. There was no way I could find my intended wife sitting and waiting for her to appear on my doorstep. I needed to take steps toward finding her. On the February 12, 2012, while recovering from a shoulder operation I'd undergone the day before that was meant to alleviate the ongoing issue of arthritis, I signed up for a dating service I could access on my cell phone.

The same day, I met a woman named Gay. She had moved to England from the Philippines and, like me, was looking for someone to develop a lasting connection with who would love her for who she was. I was drawn to her instantly and recalled thoughts I had developed years before. After turning my life over to Christ, four very specific things were placed on my heart. The first was a love for the Filipino people, which had always been present in my mind. Second was the sureness that I would, someday, marry a woman from the Philippines. Third was that she and I would have a child, and finally my heart was convicted that I would have a ministry in the Philippines at some point in my life.

Right away, Gay and I began discussing our faith in God. She was raised in a strict Roman Catholic family. I delivered my testimony to her, ministered about my journey with Jesus Christ, but never once pushed her. Even though I had strong opinions about the Catholic Church and those in Rome who controlled it, I did not want to apply any judgments or condemnations onto Gay. It is God's job to judge, not man's. She was so open to hearing my personal story and the Scriptures I shared with her, so willing and receiving, and that was enough for me. God works on all of us; it is not for me to convince or convert a single soul.

She was easy to develop affection and care for during those first conversations. For five nights in a row, Gay and I spoke via webcam for hours, getting to know one another and sharing in God's Word. After the fifth night of prayer and Scripture, she sent me a text about a particular passage that had struck her heart. Acts 2:38, which spoke of repenting of one's sins and getting baptized in the name of Jesus Christ, made a serious impression on Gay. She had been attending Catholic mass without taking communion because she wanted her life to be more in order before taking part in the sacred rite. Like I had experienced so many times in my life, Gay felt a crossroads ahead of her and was somewhat unsure of the direction she should take. I told her we could pray together when she was ready to accept Christ into her heart and ask forgiveness for her sins, and that I would be happy to say it with her when she was ready. I gently witnessed to her and showed her how God had changed my heart and my life.

On the fifth night, we said a sincere prayer from our hearts, a prayer of Gay's repentance and acceptance of Christ. She cried as she gave her life and heart to Christ. When we prayed, her tears flowed freely. After that, she asked to join me at church. My heart swelled with joy for this beautiful woman, both inside and outwardly, that I had met just days before. I had ministered to people in the past, helped lost souls find their way, but had never been so deeply invested.

We decided it was time for us to meet in person for the first time. I invited her over to my home for lunch. My arm was still in a sling from the shoulder surgery I had undergone a little over a week before, and I was unable to drive.

We spent the day cooking and enjoying chicken curry. I intended to serve a delicious salad as well, but realized too late that I didn't have any salad dressing. There was mayonnaise, however, which we put on the salad. She and I were both too polite to say how bad the mayonnaise was as salad dressing, instead picking at the salads with smiles on our faces. It was a great first date.

Two days after meeting each other in person, I received an early morning text from Gay. The text was excited but focused; God had placed it on her heart that she needed to be baptized. She had woken up that morning with the desire to be officially baptized. I introduced Gay to the pastor and congregation. The church welcomed her into the community with all the warmth I had received, and it made me deeply happy to see someone I saw a future with fitting so perfectly into my life.

Gay was the woman I wanted to marry. I trusted that fact with the surety I trusted my faith in God's Word. I had wasted too much time in my old life to hesitate again. There was a chance that Gay would need to return to the Philippines, and I would not let that happen without showing her what she meant to me. If she had to leave England, she would do so with the knowledge that I loved her.

On the 29th of February, less than a month after meeting Gay through the dating service, I booked a trip to Paignton, a romantic seaside location known for its quiet, scenic atmosphere. The hotel I chose, the Cherry Tree, is painted a whimsical pink color that reminded me of the bright pink jacket Gay had been wearing the first time I saw her in person. I planned the trip around her birthday; we would be in Paignton from March 10-12 for a holiday after the Sabbath.

I had some concern that Gay would turn the trip down. She hated to miss work, was diligent and responsible in her commitment to earning a good living and building her life. She had only known me for a short time, and it would be understandable if a few people in Gay's life would be wary of her traveling alone with me. As it turns out, the woman she rented her accommodations from had spoken out against her joining me on the holiday, had told her it was dangerous and reckless. Gay felt the connection that I felt, though, and agreed to join me on the short holiday at the shore. I was overjoyed and moved forward with my plans to propose marriage.

I wanted Gay to choose her own engagement ring. Instead of making that choice without her, I purchased an eternity ring for her to wear when she, I hoped, became my fiancée. Then, I could take her to a jewelry store in Paignton to choose her official ring. Next in my planning, I made reservations at a nice Italian restaurant and arranged with the hotel to have our room decorated with rose petals when we returned from dinner. The proposal would take place at some point during the meal.

I was nervous, but we were happy. Every conversation brought us closer together and added to the quick comfort we had developed. Then, during the special dinner date I had so carefully planned, it was time to ask Gay to be my wife. I stood up and got the attention of the dining room, which was full of other diners enjoying a quiet holiday. I expressed my love for Gay to the entire room before kneeling down beside her.

"Would you be willing to marry me?" I asked her, an anxious but genuine grin spread across my face.

Gay accepted the proposal and the symbolic eternity ring I had presented to her. That moment ranks as one of the happiest of my life, in company among moments in which I felt the true presence of God and the birth of my son. To be blessed with the love, respect, and companionship of such a sweet, beautiful, and remarkable woman was a gift from God I never could have truly dreamt of. After dinner, we returned to the hotel room. Gay was surprised by the rose petals and chocolate covered strawberries the hotel staff had arranged in the room. That night, I gave Gay her birthday gift, a King James Bible bound in pink and brown leather, which I had inscribed to her with love and blessings. She was ecstatic and grateful, as I was at her reaction to the gift.

The rest of the trip went as perfectly as I could have hoped for. Small moments of tension, the result of traveling together for the first time more often than not, were easily dispelled with prayer and the reading of God's Word. There would be work to do when we went home, important and, at times, complex steps toward marriage. That weekend was all about relaxing and enjoying our time together.

Before marrying, Gay and I decided to seek counseling and guidance from the pastor. My future wife was not only preparing for married life, but she was also working toward her baptism. The advice of the pastor, such a well-versed man of God, would prove to be extremely helpful through the process of Gay's baptism and our impending marriage.

The chance that our ability to get married would be taken away by strict immigration officials and that Gay would be asked to leave England was very real and mounting. First, there were the interviews to prove we were in love, intended to have a legitimate marriage, and were not trying to trick the system into awarding Gay the right to stay in the country. I printed out every email and every text message, no matter how personal, to prove the genuine nature of our relationship. We both knew the speed of our courtship would raise an eyebrow but hoped the honesty with which we presented our case would outshine that possible issue.

The wedding plans moved forward alongside the process of planning Gay's baptism, which would happen before we exchanged our vows in marriage before God. Gay was dedicated to her new walk with Christ. I watched with beaming pride as Gay spoke in front of our congregation. With carefully chosen words but a confident tone, she delivered her own testimony, sharing how she had turned away from the Catholic religion that she had been raised in for 39 years. Then, on April 28, Gay was baptized as a public testimony of her faith in Christ. My love and I were both baptized at the age of 39, a parallel that, to both of us, was another sign from God that we were meant to come into each other's lives.

Another victory came when Gay passed the English language proficiency exam. She narrowly made it into the May 12th exam group, a single spot opening up for her at the last minute. The two weeks we waited for the test results were tense, culminating in profound relief when we found out that not only had she received a passing grade, she had done remarkably well. One more step toward our goal, all while piecing together our wedding ceremony and reception. Discussions on citizenship interviews and bridesmaid dresses intermingled, adding happiness and light to a situation that could test the faith of the most devout. In our hearts, we knew that God had a plan for her and me, for us as a couple, and all we could do was pray and move forward.

On May 28, 2012—my birthday—Gay and I were married. The greatest reward for the changes I had made in my life, a miraculous blessing dressed in angelic white, met me at the altar and became my wife. As we recited our vows, worries about the future fled, and there was only love, hope, and happiness. I felt not only the support of the friends and family in attendance, but also that of my dear mother Grace surrounding us that day.

The next months would be difficult at times, figuring out how to pay bills and afford the expenses of keeping Gay in the country, in our home, but we faced each hurdle with God at our side lending us strength. I sold my fishing kit, a physical reminder of every relaxing sober day spent fishing and every exciting catch made in a variety of competitive matches. There was no sadness when I let the kit go, however.

I am no longer a fisher of fish, I thought to myself. I am a fisher of men. All glory to God.

For more information about

DAVID DALY
&
ONE WAY TO GRACE
please visit:

Website: onewaytograce.com
Email: onewaytograce@gmail.com
Twitter: @OneWaytoGrace
Facebook: www.facebook.com/onewaytograce

....

For more information about
AMBASSADOR INTERNATIONAL
please visit:

www.ambassador-international.com
@AmbassadorIntl
www.facebook.com/AmbassadorIntl